# favourite recipes 2

Produced by
**Women for Mission
Free Church of Scotland**

Cover design by Viewfield Design  Tel: 0141 776 0500
*featuring the Free North, St Vincent Street and Lochinver Free Churches*

Design and print Viewfield Design - www.viewfielddesign.com

*November 2005*

Published by Viewfield Design
ISBN Nos  978-0-09551764-0-1     0-9551764-0-9

# contents

# foreword

*Favourite Recipes 2* has been produced by Women For Mission, the women's association of the Free Church of Scotland, following the great success and enduring popularity of *Favourite Recipes*, published in 1994. More than ten years on, this publication has raised over £35,000 to help those whose lives have been affected by famine, war or other tragedy in different areas of the world. It is hoped that *Favourite Recipes 2* will also raise a significant sum for Disaster Relief.

The WFM want to thank most sincerely all those who have worked together in the preparation of the book:

- the friends who generously loaned the necessary finance
- the congregational representatives and presbytery co-ordinators who collected and typed the recipes
- the recipe testers who cooked, sampled and recorded their results
- those who helped prepare the copy for the printers and in particular Margaret Smith
- all those who were involved in the proof reading
- all those who helped with the distribution
- Ronnie and Graeme from Viewfield Design for their hard work, advice and patience

Thank you to everyone who took the time to send in a recipe, making this exciting new book possible. More than 900 recipes were received from over 100 congregations. Unfortunately, in a project of this kind, it is impossible to use all the contributions received. Please do not feel that you have contributed in vain if your particular recipe has not been included. Taking into account the fact that many who purchase this second book will already have the first book, the editing team decided to have as different a selection of recipes as possible. It was also our aim to try to include at least one from every congregation that participated. The recipes have come from the length and breadth of the United Kingdom, from Northern Ireland, Canada, South Africa, Peru and Colombia, as well as some from international students studying in Scotland.

Thank you also to all who have bought this book. We hope that these favourite recipes will help you to enjoy cooking and will soon prove to be your favourites too.

In an unequal world where many are in want, let us think of the poor and pray for them when we use this book to make delicious meals for our family and friends. Remember Jesus' words in Matthew's Gospel, "I was hungry and you gave me something to eat.........whatever you did for one of the least of these brothers of mine, you did for me."

**Christine Mackenzie**
President

*November 2005*

# starters

## Avocado, Mango and Prawn Salad

Serves: 6

*Dressing*
1"/2.5cm fresh ginger, grated
2 floz/50ml vegetable oil
1 floz/25ml olive oil
juice of ½ lime
pinch of caster sugar
salt and freshly ground pepper

1 bag mixed salad leaves
1 avocado, sliced
12 oz/350g cooked prawns
1 medium or ½ large mango, sliced

1. Thoroughly mix all dressing ingredients together, either in blender, or by shaking well in clean jar with lid.
2. Taste and add more lime juice, sugar or ginger if necessary.
3. Make a mound of lettuce leaves on serving plate.
4. Gently layer avocado, prawns and mango on top.
5. Trickle dressing over salad.

*Marina MacLeod, Livonia, USA*

## Creamy Mushrooms

Serves: 4-6

1 tbs oil
1-2 cloves garlic, crushed
10 oz/275g mushrooms, thinly sliced

1 tsp dried parsley
15 floz/425ml single cream
4 slices bread

1. Heat oil in pan and sauté garlic.
2. Add mushrooms and fry for 1-2 minutes.
3. Add parsley and mix in cream.
4. Toast bread.
5. Simmer sauce and serve with toast.

*Sara A MacLean, Barvas, Lewis*

# Chicken Liver Paté

Serves: 6-8

1 onion, chopped
2 oz/50g butter
8 oz/225g tub chicken livers

salt and pepper
1 tsp mixed herbs
1 tsp chopped parsley
2 tbs brandy or sherry

1. Sauté onion in butter. Do not brown.
2. Add chicken livers and sauté for 5-10 minutes, adding more butter if too dry.
3. Add salt, pepper, herbs, parsley, brandy or sherry.
4. Cook all together for 2 minutes and liquidize.
5. Leave to cool and serve with toast.

*Cathie Macleod, Scourie*

# Creamy Scallops with Wild Rice

Serves: 4

1 oz/25g wild rice
2 oz/50g long grain white rice
salt and pepper
$^1/_2$ oz/10g butter
1 tbs oil
1 small onion, finely chopped
2 oz/50g button mushrooms, wiped and sliced

$^1/_4$ tsp paprika
8 oz/225g scallops
2 floz/55ml dry white wine
1 tsp chopped parsley
2 floz/55ml double cream

1. Cook wild rice in plenty of boiling, salted water for 20 minutes and drain. Keep warm.
2. Cook long grain rice as above for 10 minutes and drain. Mix with wild rice, season to taste and keep warm.
3. Melt butter and oil in frying pan, add onion and mushrooms and cook for 5 minutes. Stir in paprika and cook for further 2 minutes.
4. Add scallops, wine and parsley and simmer until scallops are tender, turning them frequently. Remove scallops from pan and keep warm.
5. Add cream to pan, season to taste and simmer for approximately 2 minutes, until sauce thickens. Return scallops to pan and reheat.
6. Spoon mixture into centre of 4 scallop shells and arrange rice around edge to form a border.
7. Serve at once.

*Jess Skinner, Stornoway, Lewis*

# Quick Fish Paté

Serves: 8-10

2 oz/50g butter

salt and pepper

2 x 6 oz/175g cans tuna or salmon

I clove garlic, crushed

zest and juice of $^1/_2$ lemon

1 $^1/_2$ oz/35g fresh breadcrumbs, optional

$^1/_4$ cucumber

1. In saucepan, over low heat, gently melt butter with salt and pepper.
2. In bowl, mash tuna or salmon with fork.
3. Add crushed garlic, lemon zest and juice, melted butter and breadcrumbs.
4. Liquidize for a smoother paté if desired.
5. Transfer to serving dish, arranging peeled half slices of cucumber across top. Cover with foil or clingfilm and leave to chill in fridge for 6-8 hours.
6. Serve with lemon wedges, hot toast fingers, plain bread or crackers and a green salad.

*Trish Gibbons, Lairg*

# Smoked Salmon & Dill Tartlets

Pre-heat oven to: 200°C/400°F/Gas6    Time in oven: 30 minutes in total    Serves: 6

I lb/450g shortcrust pastry

7 oz/200g smoked salmon

2 eggs

2 tbs chopped dill, plus a few sprigs

$^1/_2$ pt/300ml carton single cream

wedges of lime

1. Cut pastry into 6 pieces. (See page no 137) Roll out and line six 4"/10cm shallow tart tins. Line with round of greaseproof paper and layer of baking beans or dry pasta.
2. Set tins on baking sheet, bake for 10 minutes, take from oven and remove paper and beans.
3. Return to oven for approximately 5 minutes, until golden. Remove and reduce oven temperature to 180°C/350°F/Gas4.
4. Cut salmon into strips and divide among tartlets.
5. Whisk eggs and dill and whisk in cream, salt and pepper. Pour into tartlets.
6. Bake for 15 minutes, until filling has set and top is pale gold.
7. Serve warm with lime wedges and dill sprigs.
8. Cool, wrap in foil and chill. If freezing, store for up to a month. Defrost before reheating.

*Note: To reheat, place in preheated oven at 180°C/350°F/Gas4 for 10 minutes.*

*Jennifer Macleod, Buccleuch & Greyfriars*

# soups

## Beetroot Borsch

Serves: 6-8

1 tbs olive oil
1 leek, finely chopped
1 celery stick, finely chopped
10 oz/275g raw beetroot, peeled and finely grated
1 potato, diced
1 carrot, finely grated

2 pt/1.2litre chicken stock
2 tsp red wine vinegar
1 tsp sugar
2 tbs soured cream

1. Heat oil in large pan and stir-fry leek and celery for 2-3 minutes until softened.
2. Add beetroot, potato and most of carrot, reserving some for garnish.
3. Add stock, season and bring to the boil.
4. Reduce heat and simmer, stirring occasionally, for about 40 minutes or until vegetables are tender and soup has thickened slightly.
5. Season and add vinegar and sugar. Heat gently until dissolved.
6. Serve with swirl of cream and reserved grated carrot.

*Note: If desired, soup may be liquidized before adding cream.*

*Violet Macdonald, Tain*

## Cauliflower and Bacon Soup

Serves: 4

1 large onion
8 rashers bacon, chopped
2 tbs vegetable oil
2 potatoes, chopped
1 small cauliflower, cut into florets

1 pt/570ml vegetable stock
1/2 pt/300ml milk
salt and pepper

1. Fry onion and bacon in oil for 2-3 minutes.
2. Stir in potatoes and cauliflower, add stock and bring to the boil.
3. Cover and simmer for 15 minutes until tender.
4. Liquidize soup and add milk.
5. Reheat gently and season to taste.

*Optional: Grill 2 rashers of bacon and crush on top.*

*Heather Macdonald, Lonemore, Skye*

# Courgette Soup

Serves: 2-3

1 oz/25g butter
1 onion, chopped
1 clove garlic, crushed
1 level tsp cumin

5 oz/150g potato, diced
12 oz/350g courgettes, sliced thickly
3/4 pt/425ml stock
1/4 pt/150ml cream
salt and pepper

1. Melt butter in pan, add onion, garlic and cumin and cook gently for a few minutes.
2. Add potatoes and courgettes and cook for a further few minutes before adding stock.
3. Bring to the boil, cover and simmer gently for 20-25 minutes or until vegetables are tender.
4. Liquidize, season and add cream before serving.

*Joan Maclennan, Kiltarlity*

# French Beef and Tomato Soup

Serves: 4+

beef on the bone
chopped onions
chopped garlic

14 oz/400g can chopped tomatoes
packet or can of Passata
beef stock cube
bay leaf
boiling water
seasoning

1. Brown a chunk of beef on the bone. Brown chopped onions lightly.
2. Add as much chopped garlic as you fancy!
3. Add tomatoes, Passata, stock cube and bay leaf.
4. Add boiling water until consistency looks right!
5. Season to taste and simmer for about 1 hour.
6. Remove bay leaf.
7. Take meat out of pan and remove bone.
8. Chop meat back into soup in small pieces and serve.

*Note: Experiment with quantities. This easy recipe works every time and is always popular! It was obtained from a chef in France, hence the lack of quantities.*

*Cath Humphries, Dingwall*

9

# Vichyssoise Soup

Serves: 4-6

3 medium-sized leeks
2 oz/50g butter
3 medium potatoes, diced
I medium green pepper, diced
I ¹/2 pt/850ml chicken stock

salt and pepper
¹/4 pt/150ml double cream
chives or spring onions, as garnish

1. Wash and chop white parts of leeks only.
2. Melt butter in pan and cook leeks slowly for 10-15 minutes without letting them brown.
3. Add potatoes, green pepper and stock.
4. Season, cover pan and simmer for 30 minutes until potatoes are soft.
5. Liquidize and add cream.
6. Serve chilled, garnished with chives or finely cut spring onions.

*Note: Can reheat and serve hot, but do not boil.*

*George Fraser, Kingussie*

# Broccoli Cream Cheese Soup

Serves: 4-6

8 oz/225g head of broccoli
I ¹/2 oz/35g butter
2 whites of leek, chopped
I medium onion, chopped
6 oz/175g Philadelphia cheese

2 tbs fine oatmeal
I pt/600ml milk
I pt/600ml vegetable stock
salt and pepper

1. Trim broccoli into ¹/4"/5mm florets, chop stalks small and set to one side.
2. Melt butter and add leeks, onion and broccoli stalks.
3. Stir, cover and simmer for 10 minutes.
4. Stir in oatmeal. Add milk, a little at a time, stirring well after each addition.
5. Add vegetable stock and salt and pepper then simmer for 10 minutes.
6. Leave to cool. Steam broccoli florets for 4 minutes.
7. Pour soup and soft cheese into food processor and blend until smooth.
8. Return to pan, add steamed broccoli florets and reheat gently.

*Mary B. MacLeod, Knock, Point, Lewis*

# Cream of Celeriac Soup

Serves: 4

2 red onions, roughly chopped
2 tbs olive oil
2 courgettes, sliced
1 carrot, sliced
1 celeriac, roughly cut up

salt
paprika
2 tbs half fat crème fraîche
fresh basil or parsley

1. Sauté onions in oil and add courgettes, carrot and celeriac.
2. Season, then add boiling water to cover.
3. Cook for about 20 minutes or until tender.
4. Liquidize along with a generous amount of herbs.
5. Add crème fraîche, check seasoning and consistency and serve hot.

*Morag Miller, St Peter's, Dundee*

# Lettuce Soup

Serves: 4

2 large onions, diced finely
2 large potatoes, diced finely
1 oz/25g butter
1 large iceberg lettuce, shredded

$^3/_4$ pt/425ml milk
$^1/_2$ pt/300ml chicken stock
salt and pepper
4 tbs fresh double cream, optional

1. Fry onions and potatoes gently in butter in pan for 5 minutes. Do not allow to brown.
2. Add lettuce and stir well. Add milk and stock.
3. Bring to the boil, stirring continuously. Cover and simmer very gently for 10-15 minutes.
4. Liquidize, return to pan, season and reheat.
5. Ladle into 4 warm soup bowls and swirl on 1 tbs cream and garnish with parsley.

*Cena Gray, Dowanvale, Glasgow*

# Tuna Chowder

Serves: 2-4

I oz/25g butter
I oz/25g plain flour
¹/2 -2 tsp curry powder
¹/2 pt/300ml warm milk

¹/2 pt/300ml chicken stock
II ¹/2 oz/326g can sweetcorn, drained
8 oz/225g can tuna, flaked
parsley, chopped
I-2 cream crackers, optional

1. Melt butter in pan and add flour and curry powder.
2. Cook for 1-2 minutes. Add warm milk, stirring continuously.
3. Add stock, sweetcorn and tuna.
4. Bring to the boil, simmer for 5 minutes and add parsley.
5. Pour into individual soup bowls and sprinkle crushed crackers on top.

*Nita Cruickshank, Burghead*

# Spicy Butternut Squash and Apple Soup

Serves: 6

3 tbs butter
I onion, chopped
I clove garlic, crushed
I ¹/2 lb/700g butternut squash
3 Granny Smith apples

I pt/600ml chicken stock from stock cubes
I-2 tsp ground cumin
2 tbs crème fraîche
I red apple

1. Melt butter in soup pan and fry onions and garlic.
2. Peel, seed and cut butternut squash and apples into chunks. Add to onions.
3. Pour in stock, bring to the boil and simmer on low heat for 15 minutes.
4. Stir in cumin, season and liquidize.
5. Reheat before serving and add crème fraîche.
6. Garnish with finely chopped red apple.

*Ella MacDonald, Knockbain*

 # salads

## Spinach and Carrot Salad

Serves: 6-8

12 oz/350g baby leaf spinach
12 oz/350g carrots, grated
8 oz/225g cucumber, cubed

*Dressing*
1 clove garlic, crushed
1 tbs wine vinegar
4 tbs olive oil
2 tsp clear honey
2 tsp soy sauce
salt and pepper
1 oz/25g flaked almonds, toasted

1. Mix vegetables together and place in serving bowl.
2. Mix dressing ingredients together, pour over and toss.
3. Sprinkle toasted flaked almonds on top.

*J. Anderson, Buccleuch & Greyfriars, Edinburgh*

## Chinese Love Salad

Serves: 4

1 small to medium bag baby spinach
7 oz/200g bean sprouts, fresh
2 oz/50g cooked rice
3 oz/75g red pepper, chopped
3 oz75g green onion, chopped
4 oz/110g broken cashews
6 oz/175g sultanas
1 can mandarin oranges

*Dressing*
2 tbs soya sauce
2 floz/50ml oil
2 garlic cloves, chopped

1. Place dressing ingredients in small covered container and shake.
2. Place all other ingredients in large bowl and mix together.
3. Add dressing about 1 hour before serving.

*Joyce MacFadyen, Cape Traverse, P.E.I.*

salads

# Cous Cous Salad

Serves: 4

14 floz/400ml vegetable stock
1/4 tsp ground turmeric
1/4 tsp paprika
1/4 tsp ground coriander
6 oz/175g cous cous

2 tomatoes, diced
1 red pepper, seeded and finely diced
2 spring onions, finely chopped
2 tbs chopped fresh mint
2 tbs chopped fresh parsley
juice of 1/2 lemon
salt and freshly ground black pepper

1. Bring stock to the boil in saucepan, add spices and cous cous and stir well.
2. Remove from heat and cover with lid for 1 minute.
3. Pour cous cous into large bowl, add vegetables, herbs and seasoning and mix well.
4. Just before serving, drizzle with lemon juice. Serve hot or cold.

*Note: Chopped bacon may be added if desired.*

*Joan Lipp, Rosskeen*

# Crunchy Romaine Toss

Serves: 8-10

9 oz/200g plain instant noodles
8 oz/225g chopped walnuts
2 oz/50g butter
1 head broccoli
1 head romaine lettuce
4 spring onions, chopped

*Sweet and Sour Dressing*
4 floz/125ml vegetable oil
3 1/2 oz/100g sugar
2 floz/75ml red wine vinegar
1/2 tbs soy sauce
salt and pepper

1. Break up noodles.
2. Brown walnuts and noodles in butter and cool.
3. Chop broccoli into bite-sized pieces.
4. Wash lettuce and break into pieces.
5. Combine all ingredients, pour dressing over salad and toss.

*Jennifer Richard, St Columba's, Edinburgh*

# Pasta Salad with Peppers

Serves: 4-6

I lb/450g pasta bows
I red pepper, diced
I green pepper, diced

3 spring onions, chopped
salt and pepper
4 tbs mayonnaise

1. Cook pasta according to packet instructions.
2. Drain, rinse under cold running water and leave to cool.
3. Put pasta into salad bowl and add peppers, onions, salt and pepper.
4. Add mayonnaise and stir well.
5. Chill, ready to serve in 20 minutes.

*Caroline Campbell, Lonemore*

# Pineapple Madras Salad

Serves: 4

4 slices pineapple, diced
I oz/25g sultanas
$^1/_4$ pt/150ml pineapple juice
$^1/_2$ tsp curry powder
$^1/_2$ tsp ginger powder

2 oz/50g cucumber, diced
I tomato, diced
I stick celery
$^1/_4$ pt/150ml natural yoghurt

1. Poach pineapple and sultanas in pineapple juice with spices for 2 minutes
2. Leave to cool.
3. Add cucumber, tomato and celery. Strain and divide between 4 plates.
4. Combine a little juice with yoghurt and drizzle over salad.

*Dorothy Ross, Hilton, Fearn*

# Broccoli Salad

Serves: 4-6

8 slices bacon
I head broccoli
I onion, chopped finely
I teacup cheese, grated

$^1/_2$ teacup mayonnaise
$^1/_4$ teacup sugar
I tbs vinegar

1. Place bacon in frying pan with no oil, fry until crisp then chop into small pieces.
2. Break head of broccoli into very small florets. Peel and grate stems.
3. Mix together bacon, broccoli, onion and cheese.
4. Stir mayonnaise, sugar and vinegar together and pour over broccoli mix.
5. Make the day before and keep refrigerated.

*Anne MacIver, Resolis & Urquhart*

 # vegetarian

## Broccoli Quiche

Pre-heat oven to: 200°C/400°F/Gas6     Time in oven: 35-40 mins in total     Serves: 6-8

8 oz/225g shortcrust pastry      1 large onion, chopped
8 oz/225g broccoli florets      1 oz/25g butter
3 large eggs      3 oz/75g cheddar cheese, grated
1/2 pt/300ml single cream
salt and pepper

1. Roll out pastry to line a 9"/23cm diameter flan tin. (See page no 137)
2. Cover with greaseproof paper and layer of baking beans. Bake for 10-15minutes.
3. Remove paper and beans and return flan to oven for 5 minutes.
4. Reduce oven temperature to 180°C/350°F/Gas4.
5. Blanch broccoli in boiling water for 2 minutes and allow to cool.
6. Beat eggs and cream together and add salt and pepper.
7. Fry onions lightly in butter, put in pastry case and cover with broccoli.
8. Pour in eggs and grated cheese.
9. Sprinkle with small amount of grated cheese.
10. Bake for about 20 minutes until filling is set.
11. Serve hot or cold.

*C. Mackenzie, Kilwinning*

## Cheese Soufflé

Pre-heat oven to: 200°C/400°F/Gas6     Time in oven: 25 minutes     Serves: 4

2 oz/50g butter      5 oz/150g cheese
1 1/2 oz/35g flour      salt and cayenne pepper
1/2 pt/300ml milk      4 eggs

1. Over a gentle heat, melt butter in saucepan. Stir in flour and cook for 2 minutes.
2. Gradually add milk, stirring continuously, and simmer for a few minutes.
3. Add cheese and season. Cool slightly.
4. Separate eggs, add yolks to sauce and beat to a smooth consistency.
5. Whisk whites until stiff and fold in.
6. Gently pour mixture into a greased 3 pt/1.7litre soufflé dish.
7. Cook until well risen and brown on the top.

*Note: May also be served as a starter.*

*George Fraser, Kingussie*

# Cauliflower and Nut Flan

Pre-heat oven to: 180°C/350°F/Gas4     Time in oven: 30-35 minutes     Serves: 3-4

I pastry flan case

2 eggs, lightly beaten

4 floz/125g milk

3 oz/75g walnuts, chopped

4 oz/110g grated cheddar cheese

salt and pepper

I onion, finely chopped

I oz/25g butter

I cauliflower, chopped

2 tomatoes, peeled and chopped

1. Make a 9"/23cm shortcrust pastry flan case. (See page no 137)
2. Beat together eggs, milk, walnuts, cheese, salt and pepper until well blended.
3. Fry onion in butter, until soft, and add to egg mixture.
4. Arrange cauliflower in bottom of flan case and cover with tomatoes.
5. Pour egg mixture over and bake until golden brown.

*Bunty Matheson, Nairn*

# Kidney Bean Bake

Serves: 4

14 oz/400g can chopped tomatoes

14 oz/400g can red kidney beans

I large onion, chopped

I clove garlic, crushed

dash of red wine, optional

2 oz/50g breadcrumbs

2 oz/50g grated cheese

1. Simmer tomatoes, beans, onions, garlic and wine in pan until onions are soft.
2. Mash with potato masher.
3. Place in a heatproof dish, cover with breadcrumbs and grated cheese.
4. Brown under grill.

*Ann Slater, Glendale, Skye*

# Cuban Fried Bananas

Serves: 4

8 oz/225g long grain rice

4 bananas

butter or oil for frying

I large mango

15 oz/420g can red kidney beans

1. Cook rice as per instructions and allow to cool.
2. Cut bananas in long diagonals, frying to a nice crisp, as you would fried potatoes.
3. Peel mango and chop finely.
4. Drain kidney beans and add to rice with chopped mango.
5. Serve with bananas and a green salad.

*Kenna Macdonald, Ness, Lewis*

# Mushroom Bake

Pre-heat oven to: 190°C/375°F/Gas5     Time in oven: 30 minutes     Serves: 2-3

6 oz/175g wholemeal breadcrumbs

4 oz/110g margarine

2 oz/50g chopped mixed nuts

1 small onion grated

4 oz/110g cheese grated

grated rind and juice of $1/2$ lemon

1 tbs parsley

8 oz/225g mushrooms, sliced

1 lb/450g tomatoes, chopped

salt and pepper

1. Place breadcrumbs in a bowl and rub in 3oz/75g of margarine.
2. Mix in nuts, onion, cheese, lemon rind and parsley.
3. Press half of this mixture into a greased casserole dish.
4. Melt remaining margarine in pan, fry mushrooms for 5 minutes and add to casserole dish.
5. Cover mushrooms with chopped tomatoes and season.
6. Add remaining mixture and press down firmly. Bake in oven.

*Attie MacRae, Poolewe & Aultbea*

# Vegetable Rice Bake

Pre-heat oven to: 200°C/400°F/Gas6     Time in oven: 20 minutes     Serves: 12

1 $1/2$ lb/700g brown rice

1 oz/25g margarine

8 oz/225g onions, chopped

4 oz/110g red peppers, sliced

8 oz/225g carrots, diced

8 oz/225g small florets of cauliflower

8 oz/225g frozen peas

1 lb/450g cheese, grated

salt and pepper

$1/2$ tsp paprika

1 dsp mixed herbs

8 oz/225g tomatoes, sliced.

1. Boil rice and drain. Melt margarine, fry onions and peppers and cook until tender.
2. Mix together all ingredients except tomatoes and half the cheese.
3. Put in a greased, deep oven-proof dish.
4. Place sliced tomatoes on top and cover with remainder of cheese.
5. Place in oven and cook until mixture is bubbling and cheese is browned.
6. Serve with salad, crusty bread and new potatoes.

*Margaret MacAulay, Cross, Ness, Lewis*

# Squash and Chickpea Casserole with Herby Dumplings

Pre-heat oven to: 160°C/325°F/Gas3    Time in oven: 35 minutes    Serves: 8

*Casserole*

2 tbs olive oil

I onion, chopped

2 garlic cloves, crushed

2 lb/900g butternut squash, chopped

2 x 14 oz/400g can chopped tomatoes

2 x 14 oz/400g can chickpeas, drained

¹/₂ pt/300ml vegetable stock

I tsp mixed herbs, dried

chopped parsley for garnish

*Dumplings*

4 oz/110g S.R. flour

salt and pepper

I tsp mixed herbs

2 oz/50g vegetarian suet or margarine

7-8 tbs cold water

*Casserole*
1. Heat oil in suitable casserole over medium heat.
2. Add onion, garlic and squash and cook for 5-10 minutes.
3. Add chickpeas, stock, herbs, seasoning and tomatoes and simmer for 15 minutes.

*Dumplings*
1. Sift flour and add seasoning and herbs.
2. Stir in suet and cold water to make a soft dough.
3. Divide into 8 pieces and shape lightly into balls. Add to casserole.
4. Cover and bake for 15 minutes. Remove cover and cook for further 20 minutes, until dumplings are golden and vegetables are tender.
5. Serve garnished with parsley.

*Ella MacDonald, Golspie*

# Vegetarian Roast

Pre-heat oven to: 220°C/425°F/Gas7    Time in oven: 10-15 minutes    Serves: 4

4 red peppers

8 tomatoes, halved or sliced

salt and pepper

basil, optional

8 oz/225g grated cheese

olive oil

1. Cut peppers in half lengthwise, removing seeds and pith.
2. Put 2 tomato halves or slices in each half pepper and sprinkle with salt, pepper and basil.
3. Spread layer of cheese over tomatoes.
4. Place in oiled roasting dish, drizzle a little olive oil on each and place in oven.
5. Serve with garlic bread.

*Murdo Morrison, St Columba's, Edinburgh*

# Tagliatelle with Mushrooms and Stilton

Serves: 4

I lb/450g tagliatelle verdi
3 oz/75g button mushrooms
6 oz/175g Stilton or Gruyère cheese

I ¹/₂ oz/35g butter
2 small cloves garlic, crushed
10 floz/300ml double cream
parsley

1. Cook tagliatelle as per instructions on packet.
2. Thinly slice mushrooms and crumble/grate cheese.
3. Melt butter in saucepan, add garlic and stir in mushrooms.
4. Add double cream and heat gently, but do not boil. Mixture will be quite runny.
5. Add cheese and heat through.
6. Remove from heat and transfer to blender. Blend for I minute.
7. Drain pasta, return to pan, add sauce and stir.
8. Place in serving dish and garnish with parsley.

*Margaret M Mackay, Bettyhill*

# Onion Tart

Pre-heat oven to: 200°C/400°F/Gas6        Time in oven: 35 mins in total     Serves: 6-8

I roll short crust pastry
2 oz/50g butter
I tbs olive oil
I ¹/₂ lb/700g onions, sliced

2 whole eggs
2 egg yolks
5 floz/150ml single cream
salt and pepper
nutmeg, freshly grated

1. Roll out pastry, line a flan ring 8"/20cm and refrigerate for 20 minutes.
2. Melt butter in large frying pan. Add oil and onions and sauté slowly until soft, for about 30 minutes. Allow to cool.
3. Take pastry case out of fridge, line with round of greaseproof paper and baking beans or dry pasta.
4. Bake for 10 minutes, take from oven and remove paper and beans.
5. Return to oven for approximately 5 minutes, until golden.
6. Reduce oven temperature to 180°C/350°F/Gas4.
7. Mix together eggs, yolks, cream and onions. Season to taste.
8. Pour into prepared flan case and sprinkle with nutmeg.
9. Bake for about 20 minutes, until golden brown.

*Lily M Campbell, Stornoway, Lewis*

# Vegetable Lasagne
Pre-heat oven to: 180°C/350°F/Gas4          Time in oven: 45 minutes          Serves: 4-6

**5 tbs olive oil**

**1 large onion, roughly chopped**

**1-2 garlic cloves, crushed**

**1 large green pepper, chopped**

**1 large red pepper, chopped**

**1 lb/450g courgettes, sliced**

**1 ¹/₂ oz/35g butter or margarine**

**1 lb/450g mushrooms, sliced**

**salt and freshly ground pepper**

**1 pt/600ml tomato sauce**

**¹/₄ tsp freshly grated nutmeg**

**1 pt/600ml coating cheese sauce**

**8 oz/225g lasagne**

**2 oz/50g Parmesan cheese, freshly grated**

**few sprigs of fresh basil**

1. Heat 2 tbs oil in heavy-based frying pan.
2. Add onion, garlic and peppers. Fry gently for about 10 minutes until they are soft. Remove from pan with slotted spoon and put into bowl.
3. Fry courgettes in batches for about 5 minutes, until slightly coloured, and turn frequently, adding more oil as necessary.
4. Remove courgettes from pan with slotted spoon and set aside in bowl with onions and peppers.
5. Melt butter in pan, add mushrooms a few at a time and fry over brisk heat until slightly coloured. Remove each batch with slotted spoon and mix with other vegetables.
6. Return all vegetables to pan and season. Mix together with tomato sauce.
7. Make cheese sauce. (See white sauce on page no 138) Add nutmeg.
8. Spoon one third of tomato sauce mixture over base of a greased 12"/30cm square baking dish. Cover with one third of cheese sauce and arrange one half of pasta on top.
9. Repeat layers of tomato, cheese sauce and pasta, ending with cheese sauce on top.
10. Sprinkle Parmesan cheese evenly on top. Bake until golden and bubbling.
11. Decorate with sprigs of basil. Serve hot with garlic bread.

*Fiona MacNicol, Fort William*

 # fish

## Crab and Ginger Tart with Chilli Dressing

Pre-heat oven to: 200°C/400°F/Gas6     Time in oven: 45-50 mins in total     Serves: 8

I lb/450g shortcrust pastry
4"/10cm fresh ginger, chopped
I oz/25g flat leaf parsley
2 tbs sunflower oil
9 oz/250g fresh or tinned white crabmeat
2 eggs
2 egg yolks
¹/₂ pt/300ml crème fraîche

*Chilli dressing*
4 spring onions, finely chopped
juice of I lime
I red chilli, chopped
3 tbs light soya sauce
6 tbs sunflower oil
I tbs caster sugar
I tbs water

1. Line a 9"/25cm loose-based, shallow tart tin with rolled-out pastry. (See page 137)
2. Chill for 15 minutes. Bake blind for 10-15 minutes.
3. Blend ginger, parsley and oil to a coarse paste and spread over base of tart.
4. Scatter crabmeat over ginger paste.
5. Whisk together eggs, yolks and crème fraîche.
6. Put tart tin on baking sheet and pour over egg mixture.
7. Bake in oven for 30-35 minutes.
8. Serve warm with chilli dressing, made by mixing all ingredients together.

*Mary Morrison, Scalpay*

## Fish Pie

Pre-heat oven to: 200°C/400°F/Gas6     Time in oven: 30-35 minutes     Serves: 4

I lb/450g smoked haddock and cod
4 tbs milk
I oz/25g butter
I oz/25g flour
¹/₄ pt/150ml apple juice

I tsp parsley, chopped
4 hard boiled eggs, roughly chopped
salt and pepper
I ¹/₄ lb/600g small potatoes, parboiled
2 tbs cooking oil

1. Poach fish in milk for 3 minutes, drain and reserve milk.
2. Melt butter in saucepan, add flour, stir and cook for I minute.
3. Gradually add milk and apple juice.
4. Continue stirring until sauce reaches boiling point.
5. Flake fish and fold into sauce along with parsley and eggs. Season to taste.
6. Transfer to oven-proof dish, arranging potatoes round edge of dish.
7. Brush with oil and bake in oven.

*Annetta Maclennan, Shawbost, Lewis*

# Haddock Soufflé
Pre-heat oven to: 190°C/375°F/Gas5     Time in oven: 40-45 minutes     Serves: 4

8 oz/225g smoked haddock fillets
1/2 pt/300ml milk
1 oz/25g butter
1 oz/25g plain flour

4 oz/110g grated cheese
juice and rind of lemon
salt and pepper
2 eggs, separated

1. Cook fish in milk for 10 minutes.
2. Remove from pan, discard skin and flake fish, reserving cooking liquid.
3. Melt butter, add flour and cook for 1 minute.
4. Gradually add reserved liquid, stirring continuously, and cook for 2 minutes.
5. Allow sauce to cool.
6. Stir in fish, cheese, lemon and seasoning.
7. Beat in egg yolks.
8. Whisk egg whites until thick, but not stiff.
9. Fold into mixture and place in a greased 1 1/4 pt/725ml oven-proof dish.
10. Bake in oven until soufflé is well risen.
11. Serve immediately with crusty bread and salad.

*Isabel Smith, Ayr*

# Kedgeree
Pre-heat oven to: 200°C/400°F/Gas6     Time in oven: 15-20 minutes     Serves: 6

6 oz/175g easy-to-cook long grain rice
12 floz/330ml boiling water
1/2 tsp salt
8 oz/225g smoked haddock fillet, skinned
8 oz/225g fresh haddock fillet, skinned

2 medium hard boiled eggs
2 oz/50g unsalted butter or margarine
1/4 pt/150ml single cream
2 tsp caster sugar
white pepper

1. Cook rice with water and salt in covered pan for 15 minutes, over a medium heat. Do not stir until end.
2. Poach smoked haddock in 2 changes of cold water to remove excess salt. Each time water should be brought to the boil and the fish simmered for 3-4 minutes, then drained.
3. Poach fresh haddock by itself for 6-10 minutes. Keep water bubbling gently. Drain.
4. Flake up both kinds of haddock with two forks.
5. Shell eggs and roughly chop.
6. Put butter, cream, sugar and pepper into large saucepan and warm gently until butter melts.
7. Lightly fork in rice, fish and eggs.
8. Transfer to a buttered heat-proof dish, leave uncovered and place in oven.

*J. M. Maclean, Cross, Ness, Lewis*

# Herring with Tarragon

Pre-heat oven to: 150°C/300°F/Gas2     Time in oven: 20-30 minutes     Serves: 4

4 herring, gutted and heads removed

salt and pepper

*Stuffing*

I orange

4 spring onions, finely chopped

2 oz/50g fresh wholemeal breadcrumbs

I tbs fresh tarragon, chopped

salt and pepper

*Garnish*

2 oranges, sliced thickly

I tbs light brown sugar

I tbs olive oil

fresh tarragon sprig

*Stuffing*
1. Grate half orange rind. Chop up orange - use processor, if available.
2. Combine orange mixture with spring onions, breadcrumbs and tarragon in bowl.
3. Season with salt and pepper.

*Fish*
1. Fill herring cavities with stuffing.
2. Place fish on lightly-oiled foil, wrap round fish and bake.
3. Flesh should be white and firm to touch when cooked.
4. Place sliced oranges on a baking tray, sprinkle with sugar and drizzle with oil. Grill to heat through.
5. Transfer fish to plates and garnish with grilled orange slices and fresh tarragon sprig.
6. Serve with salad

*Margaret Macdonald, Ness, Lewis*

# Salmon with a Creamy Dill Sauce

Serves: 4

4 salmon fillets

2 ½ tsp dried dill

salt and pepper

I tbs olive oil

I tsp English mustard

¼ pt/150ml double cream

5 ½ oz/165g carton natural yoghurt

¼ cucumber

1. Sprinkle one side of salmon with 2 tsp dill.
2. Add salt and pepper and drizzle with oil.
3. Place salmon under grill and cook for 4 minutes, grill heat 4, medium high.
4. Turn, cook for a further 4 minutes, place on serving dish and keep warm.
5. Mix mustard with ½ tsp dill and cream and bring to boil quickly.
6. Take off heat and stir in yoghurt. Return to gentle heat - do not boil.
7. Pour over salmon and garnish with thinly-sliced cucumber.
8. Serve with cooked, thinly-sliced carrots and potatoes.

*Mrs Ishbel Morrison, Perth*

# Potato and Fish Flan

Serves: 8

1 ½ lb/700g smoked haddock fillet

2 lbs/900g potatoes

2 eggs

4 oz/110g butter

1 pt/600ml milk

2 oz/50g flour

salt and pepper

4 tomatoes

2 tbs mayonnaise

1. Wash fish and simmer in water for 8-10 minutes. Drain and flake.
2. Peel and wash potatoes. Cook in boiling salted water until tender and drain and dry over low heat.
3. Place in mixer or food processor until potatoes are broken down.
4. Prepare moderate grill.
5. Separate eggs and place whites in a clean, grease-free bowl.
6. Add yolks and 2 oz/50g butter to potatoes in machine and mix well.
7. Spread potatoes over base and sides of a baking tray 12"x 8"x 1"/30cm x 20cm x 2.5cm to form case. Place under grill for 6-8 minutes until potatoes have lightly browned.
8. Blend milk and flour until smooth. Melt remaining 2 oz/50g butter in saucepan and add milk mixture. Bring to the boil, stirring continuously. Cook for 3 minutes.
9. Stir flaked fish into sauce and season to taste.
10. Slice tomatoes and place over base of potato case. Cover with fish mixture.
11. Whisk egg whites until stiff but not dry. Fold in mayonnaise and spread over fish.
12. Place under grill until just golden brown. Garnish with chopped parsley or chives.
13. Serve at once.

*Note: Half this quantity can be cooked in an 8"/20 cm round tin and will serve 4.*
*A potato masher and wooden spoon can be used instead of a food processor.*

*Elma Ross, Lochcarron*

# Monk Fish Tails

Pre-heat oven to: 180°C/350°F/Gas4     Time in oven: 11-12 minutes.     Serves: 2

¼ - ½ jar sun-dried tomatoes in oil

1 handful fresh basil

dash of balsamic vinegar

8 sheets Parma ham, 4 per piece of monkfish

2 pieces monkfish tails

1. Blitz basil, tomatoes and vinegar together to form a paste, using some of the oil.
2. Lay Parma ham on cling film or parchment paper to ease rolling up.
3. Spread with ½ paste on each, lay monkfish tail on top and roll up.
4. Place on greased oven tray and bake.

*Margaret Bruce, Elgin and Forres*

## Salmon Fillets with Caramelised Onions and Basil

Pre-heat oven to: 190°C/375°F/Gas5     Time in oven: 20-25 minutes     Serves: 4

| | |
|---|---|
| 2 tbs olive oil | 2 oz/50g sun-dried tomatoes in oil |
| 2 medium onions, peeled and chopped | 3 oz/75g fresh white breadcrumbs |
| generous pinch of sugar | 3 tbs fresh basil, finely shredded |
| 2 cloves garlic, peeled and crushed | I oz/25g Parmesan cheese, finely grated |
| | I oz/25g butter, melted |
| | salt and freshly ground black pepper |
| | 4 salmon fillets, skinned |
| | green beans to serve |
| | basil leaves to garnish |

1. Heat oil in frying pan, add onions and sugar and fry gently for 10 minutes until soft.
2. Add garlic and fry for I minute more. Drain and chop sun-dried tomatoes.
3. Mix together sun-dried tomatoes, breadcrumbs, fresh basil, cheese and melted butter in a bowl, making sure that breadcrumbs are coated in butter. Season well.
4. Place salmon fillets in shallow baking dish.
5. Spread onions over each fillet and press breadcrumb mixture on top.
6. Bake until salmon is tender and crust is golden and crispy.
7. Serve at once on a bed of green beans and sprinkle with basil.

*Mary Mackenzie, Partick, Glasgow*

## Thai Fish Cakes

Serves: 4-6

| | |
|---|---|
| I lb/450g skinless, firm cod fillets | I tbs root ginger, grated |
| I tsp crushed chilli peppers | I tsp lime rind, grated |
| I shallot, finely chopped | I tbs fish sauce |
| 2 cloves garlic, peeled and crushed | I large egg, beaten |
| 4 sprigs coriander, chopped | $\frac{1}{2}$ tsp salt |

1. Whizz cod fillets in blender or food processor until finely minced.
2. Transfer in to large mixing bowl and add all other ingredients.
3. Use hands to combine all ingredients together. The end result should be a firm sticky mixture.
4. Switch on deep fat fryer or heat oil carefully in suitable pan.
5. Divide mixture into 16 portions. With slightly wet hands, mould each portion into a round shape measuring about $\frac{1}{2}$"/1.25cm thick, taking care to smooth sides and top.
6. Deep fry each fish cake for 2-3 minutes.
7. Serve with Thai Sweet Chilli Dipping Sauce.

*Note: Fish Sauce and Thai Sweet Chilli Dipping Sauce are available in supermarkets.*

*Donna Macleod, Shawbost, Lewis*

# Smoked Haddock with Mustard Cream Sauce

Serves: 4

6 oz/175g fillets smoked haddock
$^3/_4$ pt/425ml milk
2 lb/900g potatoes, peeled
salt and pepper
I oz/25g butter

$^1/_4$ pt/150ml crème fraîche
2 tbs wholegrain mustard
parsley to garnish

1. Lay fish fillets in frying pan and cover with milk.
2. Poach fish until firm. Do not let milk boil.
3. Drain, reserve milk and put fish on a plate.
4. Cover with damp greaseproof paper to keep fish moist and keep warm in oven. Reserve milk.
5. Boil potatoes until tender, drain and mash with butter. Season to taste.
6. Add 3-5 floz/100-150ml reserved milk.
7. Heat crème fraîche with mustard in small pan. Add water or little reserved milk to make sauce-like consistency.
8. Spoon mashed potato in centre of 4 plates and lay one haddock fillet on each.
9. Spoon over mustard sauce and garnish with parsley. Serve with peas.

*Catherine Macleod, Kilmuir, Stenscholl and Snizort*

# Stuffed Salmon

Pre-heat oven to: 180°C/350°F/Gas4    Time in oven: 30-45 minutes   Serves: 10-12

6-7 lb/2.7-3.15 kg salmon
*Stuffing*
2 oz/50g white breadcrumbs
4 oz/110g almonds, unblanched
2 oz/50g parsley

I tbs thyme or tarragon
3 tbs lemon zest
2 tbs lemon juice
4 oz/110g salt butter
salt, pepper and cayenne pepper

*Stuffing*
1. Combine first 3 stuffing ingredients.
2. Blend in processor and add remaining ingredients.
3. Season to taste.

*Fish*
1. Fillet fish and pat dry.
2. Lay one side of fillet on a long length of clingfilm.
3. Place stuffing along length of fish.
4. Lay second fillet on top and wrap tightly with clingfilm.
5. Place fish on length of foil and secure loosely.
6. Lay in large roast tin and bake.
7. Serve with potatoes, lemon, butter and mixed salad.

*Nan Ferguson, Ness, Lewis*

# meat

## Cottage Pie

Pre-heat oven to: 200°C/400°F/Gas6 — Time in oven: 20-25 minutes — Serves: 6

2 tbs oil
I lb/450g minced beef
2 onions, sliced
2 carrots, diced
2 tbs fresh thyme leaves, chopped
2 tbs fresh parsley, chopped
salt and ground black pepper
I tbs plain flour
I tbs tomato purée
2 tbs Worcestershire sauce
½ pt/300ml vegetable stock

*Topping*
2 lb/900g floury potatoes, scrubbed clean
3 floz/75ml milk
2 oz/50g butter
2 small leeks, trimmed, rinsed and chopped
3 oz/75g Cheddar cheese, grated

1. Heat oil in pan, stir in minced beef and fry for 5 minutes until browned.
2. Stir onions into minced beef and fry for 5 minutes until soft.
3. Add carrots and herbs, seasoning well.
4. Stir in flour and cook for I minute.
5. Stir tomato purée and Worcestershire sauce into hot stock.
6. Add gradually to meat mixture, stirring well.
7. Continue stirring, bring to the boil, cover and simmer for 30 minutes until meat is tender.
8. Meanwhile, place potatoes in pan of water and bring to the boil. Cook for 20-25 minutes until tender. Drain potatoes, peel and discard skin.
9. Place in large bowl, mash with milk and three quarters of butter and season.
10. Spoon meat mixture into a 2½ pt/1.5 litre deep roasting tin or oven-proof dish and level the surface.
11. Spoon mashed potatoes over meat, spreading out evenly with the back of a spoon.
12. Melt remaining butter in pan, add leeks and fry for 5 minutes.
13. Sprinkle leeks and grated cheese over mashed potatoes.
14. Bake in oven until cheese is golden brown and bubbling.

*Alice MacLeod, Lochs, Lewis*

# Beef or Chicken Fajitas

Requires: 3 hours to marinate · · · · · · · · · · · · · · · Serves: 8-10

| | |
|---|---|
| 1 ¹/₂ lb/700g raw steak or chicken | 2 tbs olive oil |
| **Marinade** | 1 red pepper, sliced |
| 1 clove garlic, crushed | 1 green pepper, sliced |
| 1 ¹/₂ tsp salt | 1 onion, sliced |
| 1 ¹/₂ tsp cumin | 8-10 large flour tortillas |
| 1 tsp chilli powder | 5 oz/150g cheese, grated |
| 1 tsp red pepper flakes | 1 lettuce, shredded |
| 2 tbs olive oil | 6 tomatoes, chopped |
| 2 tbs lemon juice | 8 oz/225g salsa sauce |
| | ¹/₂ pt/300ml sour cream |

1. Cut steak or chicken into strips.
2. Stir meat into marinade ingredients in zip-lock bag or medium bowl and marinate for at least 3 hours or longer in refrigerator.
3. Heat olive oil in frying pan and stir-fry peppers and onion until tender.
4. Stir in marinated meat and fry to cook through.
5. Warm tortillas and fill with some cooked meat mixture, grated cheese, lettuce, tomato, salsa sauce and sour cream.
6. Roll up and serve with rice or salad.

*Linda MacNevin, Desable, P. E. I.*

# Meaty Fennel and Mushroom Casserole

Pre-heat oven to: 170°C/325°F/Gas3 · · · Time in oven: 2-2¹/₂ hrs in total · · · Serves: 3-4

| | |
|---|---|
| 1 lb/450g lean beef, lamb or pork, cubed | 2 tbs redcurrant jelly, or apple sauce if using pork |
| 1 onion, cut into chunks | ¹/₄ pt/150ml red wine, or white if using pork |
| 2 cloves garlic, crushed | ³/₄ pt/425ml stock |
| 5 oz/150g button mushrooms | 6 oz/175g ready-made garlic bread loaf, cut into |
| 1 fennel, cut into wedges | slices |

1. Place all ingredients, except garlic bread, in large casserole dish.
2. Mix well, cover and place in oven for approximately 1 ¹/₂ -2 hours, until meat is tender.
3. If sauce requires thickening stir in 1 tsp cornflour mixed with 2 tbs cold water and allow casserole to simmer for 5 minutes.
4. Remove casserole lid, arrange garlic bread slices on top and return to oven for a further 15 minutes.
5. Serve with steamed cabbage and mashed potato.

*Margaret MacAulay, Cross, Ness, Lewis.*

# Beef Stroganoff

Serves: 2-3

I lb/450g fillet steak
2 medium onions
9 oz/250g chestnut mushrooms
5 tbs olive oil

2 tbs paprika
pinch ground nutmeg
I tbs brandy or white wine
14 floz/400ml crème fraîche
3 tbs parsley, chopped
salt and pepper

1. Cut beef into thin strips. Cut onions into eighths and mushrooms into quarters.
2. Heat half the oil in a frying pan, fry onions for 8-10 minutes and set aside.
3. Fry mushrooms in remaining oil for 2-3 minutes and set aside.
4. Heat pan until very hot and add beef, paprika and nutmeg, frying for 2-3 minutes.
5. Add wine/brandy and allow to simmer until sauce is reduced by half.
6. Add onions, mushrooms, crème fraîche and parsley and simmer for 2-5 minutes.
7. Season and serve with rice.

*Barbara Mackenzie, Smithton-Culloden*

# Chilli Cheese Meatballs

Serves: 2

8 oz/225g lean minced beef
4 salad onions, finely chopped
2 garlic cloves, finely chopped
I red chilli, seeded and finely chopped
4 tbs Parmesan cheese, freshly grated
2 tsp thyme leaves, chopped
salt and pepper

I tbs olive oil
3 ¹/₂ floz/100ml red wine
5 oz/150g spaghetti or tagliatelle
14 oz/400g can chopped tomatoes
I bay leaf
pinch of sugar

1. Mix together mince, salad onions, garlic, chilli, 2 tbs cheese, thyme and seasoning.
2. Shape into 12 small firm balls.
3. Heat oil in large pan and fry meatballs for 3-4 minutes, shaking pan frequently until well browned.
4. Pour in red wine and bubble vigorously for 1-2 minutes.
5. Cook pasta according to packet instructions.
6. Add chopped tomatoes, bay leaf, sugar and pepper to meatballs and stir.
7. Bring to the boil and simmer for 8-10 minutes until meatballs are cooked through.
8. Drain pasta and return to pan.
9. Spoon in 4 tbs tomato sauce from the meatball mixture, tossing well together.
10. Transfer to large serving bowl, spooning meatballs and sauce on top.
11. Sprinkle remaining cheese on top and serve.

*Debbie Morrison, East Kilbride*

# Oslo Steak

Pre-heat oven to: 150°C/300°F/Gas2          Time in oven: 2 hours          Serves: 4

4 braising steaks

oil for frying

1 onion, chopped

2 tbs tomato purée

1 tsp malt vinegar

1 tsp Marmite or Bovril

1 tbs brown sugar

1 tsp Worcestershire sauce

1/2 pt/300ml beef stock

1 tsp curry powder

1 dsp cornflour

1. Fry steaks lightly in frying pan with tight lid.
2. Turn steaks after 4 or 5 minutes and repeat.
3. Place onion between steaks in casserole dish.
4. In sauce pan, bring beef stock to the boil, add tomato purée, vinegar, Marmite/Bovril, brown sugar and Worcestershire sauce, stirring continuously.
5. In a jug, mix curry powder and cornflour with a little cold water and stir in remainder of stock until it thickens slightly.
6. Pour over steaks in casserole. Cook in slow oven until tender.
7. Serve with mashed potato, or potato and turnip mashed together.

*Note: Sauce can be used to cook lamb or pork chops. Can also be made in a slow cooker.*

*Violet Macdonald, Tain*

# Beef Casserole with Orange

Pre-heat oven to: 170°C/325°F/Gas3          Time in oven: 1 1/2 hours          Serves: 6

1 1/2 lb/700g braising or rump steak

3 tbs oil

2 medium onions, chopped

2 cloves garlic, crushed

2 tbs plain flour

1/2 pt/300ml beef stock

1 orange, grated rind and juice

1 tbs tomato purée

3 tbs brandy

1 tbs treacle

salt and pepper

4 oz/110g mushrooms, chopped

1. Cut meat into 1"/2.5cm cubes and fry in half of the oil until very well browned.
2. Place meat on plate.
3. Add remaining oil and sauté onions and garlic.
4. Stir in flour and cook for 1 minute.
5. Mix together stock, orange rind and juice, tomato purée, brandy and treacle.
6. Add gradually to onions and flour, stirring well.
7. Add browned meat and season with salt and pepper.
8. Place in covered casserole dish, and simmer in slow oven until beef is tender.
9. Add mushrooms half an hour before end of cooking.

*Christine Macdonald, Dunblane*

# Spaghetti Pie

Pre-heat oven to: 180°C/350°F/Gas4     Time in oven: 25 minutes in total     Serves: 6

6 oz/175g spaghetti
2 oz/50g butter or margarine
3 oz/75g Parmesan cheese, grated
2 eggs, well beaten
salt and pepper
9 oz/250g cottage cheese

oil for frying
1 lb/450g mince
1 onion, chopped
1/2 green pepper, chopped
8 oz/225g can chopped tomatoes
6 oz/175g tomato paste or purée
1/2 tsp sugar
1 tsp dried oregano
1 tsp garlic salt
salt and pepper
4 oz/110g Mozzarella cheese, shredded

1. Cook spaghetti and drain. Stir in butter, Parmesan cheese and eggs. Season.
2. Line a buttered 10"/25.5cm pie plate with spaghetti mixture.
3. Spread cottage cheese over base.
4. While spaghetti is cooking, fry mince, onion, green pepper and meat for approximately 20 minutes until meat is browned and vegetables are tender. Drain any liquid.
5. Stir in undrained tomatoes, tomato purée, sugar, oregano and garlic salt. Bring to boiling point.
6. Pour meat mixture over spaghetti base and bake uncovered for 20 minutes.
7. Sprinkle Mozzarella cheese on top and bake for 5 minutes until cheese is melted.

*Annita Smith, Desable, P. E. I.*

# Beefburgers

Makes: 6-8

2 lb/900g steak mince
6 oz/175g beef sausage meat
1 slice of bread, crumbed
4 tbs porridge oats
2 onions, grated

1 large egg, lightly beaten
2 tsp Worcester sauce
1 tbs tomato sauce
2 tsp salt
1/4 tsp black pepper

1. Mix mince and sausage meat together with a fork.
2. Add remaining ingredients, mix well and shape into burgers. A burger press makes this task much easier.
3. Cook both sides in hot frying pan with a little oil, or under a hot grill, making sure meat is thoroughly cooked through and juices run clear.

*Note: Burgers freeze well but always use fresh mince and sausage meat, not frozen meat.*

*Dolly J. MacLeod, Barvas, Lewis*

# Steak with Pepper Sauce
Pre-heat oven to: 150°C/300°F/Gas2                           Serves: 4

**4 sirloin steaks**                          **6 floz/170ml beef stock**

**2 tsp black peppercorns, slightly crushed**    **3 tsp brandy**

**2 tsp butter**                           **6 floz/170ml double cream**

                                      **1 tsp green peppercorns, slightly crushed**

1. Rub steaks with crushed black peppercorns.
2. Heat butter in heavy based frying pan over medium heat.
3. Add steaks and fry until browned on both sides, 2 minutes per side for medium-rare and 3 minutes for medium.
4. Remove steaks and keep warm in oven.
5. Add stock and brandy to pan allowing liquid to reduce for 3-4 minutes.
6. Add cream and green peppercorns.
7. Increase heat slightly and cook, stirring until sauce thickens.
8. Remove steaks from oven, pour sauce over and serve.

*May Macdonald, Kilmuir, Stenscholl and Snizort, Skye*

# Catriona's Chicken
Pre-heat oven to: 200°C/400°F/Gas6      Time in oven: 30 minutes      Serves: 4

**4 chicken breasts, cut into bite-sized pieces**    **1 tsp chilli powder**

**olive oil**                               **1 tsp curry powder**

**selection of vegetables, e.g.**                **sprig of rosemary**

    **pre-cooked potatoes**                **2 tsp grainy mustard**

    **carrots**                              **4 tbs crème fraîche**

    **turnip**

    **courgette**

    **parsnip**

**1 garlic clove, crushed**

1. Fry chicken pieces in oil.
2. Put vegetables in large roasting tin and place chicken on top.
3. Sprinkle with chilli powder and curry powder.
4. Add sprig of rosemary, drizzle oil over all and put in oven.
5. Remove chicken and keep hot.
6. Put vegetables in serving dish and keep hot.
7. Put roasting dish on hob and add mustard and crème fraîche, mixing to make sauce.
8. Return chicken to roasting dish and heat through.
9. Serve vegetables with chicken pieces and sauce on top.

*Janet MacDonald, Tobermory*

# Chicken and Spinach Lasagne

Pre-heat oven to: 180°C/350°F/Gas4     Time in oven: 40 minutes in total    Serves: 4

*Meat Sauce*
1 oz/25g butter
1 oz/25g flour
1/2 pt/300ml milk
1/2 level tsp salt
1/4 level tsp ground nutmeg
8 oz/225g cooked chicken, minced
6 sheets lasagne

*Tomato Sauce*
1 oz/25g butter
1 large onion, finely chopped
14 oz/400g tin chopped tomatoes
1 pt/600ml water
1 chicken stock cube
3 level tbs tomato purée
8 oz/225g spinach, cooked and chopped
1 level tsp marjoram

*Topping*
2 oz/50g breadcrumbs
2 oz/50g cheddar cheese

*Meat Sauce*
1. Put butter, flour and milk in saucepan and bring slowly to the boil, stirring continuously with wooden spoon or hand whisk.
2. Add remaining meat sauce ingredients, except pasta, and stir well until mixed.

*Tomato Sauce*
1. Melt butter in large saucepan and add onion. Cook until soft, add remaining ingredients and bring to the boil. Add tomatoes and simmer for 5 minutes.
2. Pour a small amount of tomato sauce into a buttered lasagne dish and cover with 3 sheets lasagne.
3. Pour meat sauce over and cover with remaining sheets of lasagne.
4. Pour tomato sauce over.
5. Bake in centre of oven for 30 minutes.
6. Sprinkle breadcrumbs and grated cheese over top and bake for a further 10 minutes.

*Janet Smith, Coatbridge*

# Chicken Paprika

Pre-heat oven to: 180°C/350°F/Gas4     Time in oven: 30 minutes     Serves: 4

4 chicken breasts, cubed
1 onion, chopped
4 oz/110g mushrooms, sliced
1 tbs oil

12 oz/350g can Campbell's tomato soup
3 tsp paprika
2 tbs soured cream, if desired

1. Heat oil in pan and brown chicken.
2. Add onion and mushrooms to pan and cook for a few minutes.
3. Stir in soup and paprika and mix well.
4. Place in lidded casserole dish and cook in oven.
5. For a richer sauce, mix in cream before serving. Serve with boiled rice.

*Kathleen Walker, Stornoway, Lewis*

# Chicken and Bacon Salad

Serves: 2-3

| | |
|---|---|
| 2 tbs wholegrain mustard | I avocado, peeled and chopped |
| 2 tbs clear honey | I small red onion, peeled and sliced |
| 2 tbs olive oil | 4 vine tomatoes, cut in wedges |
| I garlic clove, crushed | bag of green salad mix |
| 8 rashers smoked bacon | 2 chicken breasts, cut in chunks |
| 2 thick slices crusty bread, cubed | |

1. Whisk together mustard, honey, oil and garlic and set aside.
2. Grill bacon under hot grill for 4-5 minutes and cut into bite-size pieces.
3. Place in large bowl.
4. Place bread on baking tray, drizzle with some olive oil and grill for 3-4 minutes.
5. Add to bacon.
6. Add avocado, onion, tomatoes and green salad. Mix gently together.
7. Fry chicken for 8-10 minutes until cooked and juices run clear.
8. Add dressing and bring to the boil.
9. Tip chicken and juices into bowl, toss and serve.

*Anne Maciver, Resolis & Urquhart*

# Chicken Stir-Fry

Serves: 4-6

| | |
|---|---|
| 2 tbs vegetable oil | 2 tbs cornflour |
| 4 chicken breasts | I tsp Schwartz Chinese 5 **or** 7 Spice |
| 2 onions, chopped | 4 tbs dark soya sauce |
| 8 button mushrooms, sliced | $1/2$ -I pt/300-600ml water |
| I red & I green pepper | I packet Sharwoods medium egg noodles |
| 14 oz/400g beansprouts | sesame oil, optional |
| baby sweet corn, parboiled | |
| or your own choice of vegetables | |

1. Fry chicken until cooked.
2. Add onion and cook for 2 minutes.
3. Add mushrooms and cook for 2 minutes. Add remaining vegetables and toss in wok until cooked.
4. Mix cornflour with Chinese Spice, soya sauce and water then add to wok stirring until sauce thickens.
5. Cook noodles for 4 minutes, toss in few drops of sesame oil and serve immediately.

*Note: Chinese 5 Spice is mild/medium, Chinese 7 Spice is HOT.*

*Anne MacArthur, Pairc, Lewis*

# Greek Style Baked Lemon Chicken

Pre-heat oven to: 180°C/350°F/Gas4     Time in oven: 1 ½-2 hours     Serves: 4-6

3 ½- 4 lb/1.5-1.8kg chicken, jointed

salt and pepper

4 tbs flour

olive oil for frying

2 lb/900g potatoes, peeled and thickly sliced

1 cup chicken stock or water

4 garlic cloves, crushed

1 handful chopped fresh herbs, e.g. parsley, thyme and tarragon

1 cup freshly squeezed lemon juice

1. Wipe chicken pieces clean with kitchen paper. Rub with salt and pepper and coat with flour.
2. Heat oil in a pan and fry chicken until golden.
3. Lay chicken pieces flat in shallow oven-proof dish. Fit potatoes around chicken and add stock or water.
4. Sprinkle garlic, herbs, more salt and lots of freshly ground black pepper over chicken and potatoes and pour over lemon juice.
5. Cook in oven until potatoes and chicken are tender and golden.
6. During the last hour, check to see if dish is drying out. If so, reduce temperature slightly and add some water or stock.
7. Serve with a green salad, a salad of thinly sliced tomatoes, onions and Feta/Caerphilly cheese and olives.

*Penny MacKinnon MacLeod, North Uist, Grimsay and Berneray*

# Devilled Chicken

Pre-heat oven to: 180°C/350°F/Gas4     Time in oven: 1 hour     Serves: 4

4 thighs or roasting joints of chicken

salt and freshly ground black pepper

1 tbs apricot jam

1 tsp Dijon mustard

pinch of cayenne pepper

large clove garlic, crushed

3 tbs tomato ketchup

1 tbs Worcestershire sauce

1 tbs soy sauce

1. Season joints and arrange in shallow oven-proof dish.
2. Mix jam, mustard, pepper and garlic until smooth.
3. Add tomato ketchup, Worcestershire sauce, soy sauce, salt and pepper and pour over chicken pieces, coating them evenly.
4. Place lid on dish and bake in oven.

*Margaret Gardner, Nairn*

# Creamy Chicken Curry with Cashew Nuts

Serves: 6

1 tbs oil
1 large onion, finely chopped
1 tsp root ginger, grated
1 clove garlic, minced
1 tsp chilli powder
1 tsp ground coriander
1 tsp ground cumin
1 tsp turmeric
14 floz/400ml can coconut milk
8 ½ fl oz/250ml chicken stock

4 cardamom pods, bruised
4-6 chicken breasts, in bite-size pieces
1 tbs fresh coriander leaves, chopped
5 oz/150g cashew nuts, lightly toasted
3 tbs crème fraîche

1. Heat oil in large saucepan and fry onion until soft.
2. Add ginger, garlic, chilli powder, ground coriander, cumin and turmeric and cook for 1-2 minutes.
3. Add coconut milk and stock, stirring well.
4. Add cardamom pods and chicken pieces.
5. Simmer gently for 15-20 minutes or until chicken is cooked.
6. Add cashew nuts and crème fraîche.
7. Sprinkle on chopped coriander just before serving.

*Donna MacKay, Fearn*

# Sweet and Sour Chicken

Pre-heat oven to: 170°C/325°F/Gas3     Time in oven: 1 hour     Serves: 4

½ tbs cooking oil
4 chicken breasts, sliced
2-3 sticks celery, finely chopped
½ cucumber, peeled, seeded and diced

½ pt/300ml chicken stock
5 tbs white wine
1 tbs vinegar, or wine vinegar
1 tbs soy sauce
1 tbs caster sugar
4 tbs redcurrant jelly
3 tsp cornflour, blended in little water

1. Heat oil in oven-proof casserole and fry chicken to seal it.
2. Add all other ingredients except celery and cucumber.
3. Cover with lid and cook in oven, adding celery 15 minutes from end of cooking time.
4. Serve on bed of rice with cucumber sprinkled on top.

*Elizabeth MacLauchlan, Elgin*

# Sticky Chicken Thighs

Pre-heat oven to: 190°C/375°F/Gas5     Time in oven: 35-40 minutes     Serves: 4

2 oz/50g butter

3 level tsp honey

2 large garlic cloves

8 plump chicken thighs

Cajun or Chinese 5 spice, optional

salt and pepper

1. Heat butter and honey over a low heat until just bubbling.
2. Cut garlic cloves into slivers.
3. Make 2 cuts in underside of each chicken thigh on both sides of the bone and insert a sliver of garlic. Carefully lift the skin on top and insert another piece of garlic.
4. Place joints in a roasting tin. Pour hot butter and honey mixture over each thigh.
5. Add spices and season well. Place in oven, basting occasionally.
6. Chicken is cooked when skin turns dark brown and juices run clear.
7. Discard fat from roasting tin, scrape up sticky syrup and drizzle a little over each thigh.

*Mairi MacLean, Sleat and Strath, Skye*

# Spicy Cajun Chicken Kebabs

Serves: 4

2 oz/50g creamed coconut, chopped

1 tbs dark brown sugar

1 tbs Schwartz cajun seasoning

1 tbs tomato purée

1 tbs light soy sauce

1 tbs olive oil

1 lb/450g chicken breasts, cubed

1 red pepper

1 courgette, cut into 8 pieces

8 oz/225g can pineapple chunks

*Cajun Dip*

5 floz/150ml soured cream

3 tbs mayonnaise

1 tsp Schwartz cajun seasoning

1. Dissolve coconut in 150ml boiling water and add sugar. Allow to cool.
2. In bowl, blend Cajun seasoning, tomato purée, soy sauce and oil with coconut milk.
3. Stir in chicken, cover and allow to marinate in refrigerator for at least 1 hour.
4. Thread chicken on to 4 large skewers, alternating with pepper, courgette and pineapple.
5. Place under pre-heated grill, or on a barbecue, for 15-20 minutes and turn occasionally while basting with left-over marinade.
6. Blend all dip ingredients together in small bowl. Serve with kebabs.

*Note: If Cajun spice is too hot you may use a curry powder to your taste.*

*Hazle Moore, Stranmillis, E. P. C., N. Ireland*

# Rolled Chicken Breasts with Black Pudding and Mustard Sauce

Pre-heat oven to: 200°C/400°F/Gas6        Time in oven: 45mins-1 hr        Serves: 6-8

**2 slices black pudding**
**4 chicken breasts, flattened**
**12 bacon rashers, rindless**

**Sauce**
**3 1/2 floz/100ml white wine**
**1 tbs Dijon mustard**
**5 floz/150ml double cream**

1. Grill black puddings to release fat and mash them up.
2. Place chicken breasts in a freezer bag and flatten with a rolling pin.
3. Lay flattened chicken breasts on a board and spoon some black pudding into each breast. Shape into a roll.
4. Wrap bacon round the rolled breast and secure with cocktail sticks.
5. Place chicken rolls on a greased baking tray and cook for about 1 hour.
6. Meanwhile, pour wine into small pan, reduce by a third, remove from heat and add mustard.
7. Return to heat, add cream and bring to the boil, simmering for 5 minutes until sauce thickens slightly.
8. Remove chicken from oven, slice and pour sauce over.

*Donna Macleod, Shawbost, Lewis*

# Sweet and Sour Apricot Chicken

Pre-heat oven to: 200°C/400°F/Gas6        Time in oven: 30-40 minutes        Serves: 4

**2 tbs lemon juice**
**2 tsp olive oil**
**2 cloves garlic, crushed**
**ground black pepper**
**4 skinned chicken breasts**

**4 oz/110g 'ready to eat' dried apricots**
**7 floz/200ml pure orange juice**
**1 tbs cider vinegar**
**1 level tsp brown sugar**
**1/2 level tsp ground ginger**
**1 level tsp Dijon mustard**

1. Mix lemon juice with olive oil and 1 clove garlic. Season with black pepper.
2. Put chicken in a dish, pour on lemon marinade and turn chicken breasts until coated in marinade.
3. Cover and leave in fridge for 30 minutes, turning chicken occasionally.
4. Simmer apricots in orange juice for 5-10 minutes until tender.
5. Stir in sugar, ginger, mustard, vinegar and remaining clove of garlic.
6. Simmer for a further minute. Allow to cool for 10 minutes and liquidize.
7. Arrange chicken breasts in a single layer in oven-proof dish.
8. Pour apricot glaze over chicken breasts and cover with lid.
9. Bake in oven, turning chicken occasionally.
10. Serve with Basmati and wild rice, mange tout and grilled tomatoes.

*Joan Adams, Dowanvale, Glasgow*

# Savoury Chicken and Ham Pancakes

Pre-heat oven to: 180°C/350°F/Gas4     Time in oven: 30 minutes     Serves: 4-6

| | |
|---|---|
| **Pancakes, makes 8** | **Filling** |
| 4 oz/110g plain flour | I thin slice gammon per pancake |
| pinch of salt | left-over cooked chicken or turkey |
| 2 eggs | 2-3 oz/50-75g grated cheese |
| 9 floz/250ml milk | I tsp herbs, or left-over sage and onion stuffing |
| 2 floz/50ml water | salt and pepper |
| **Sauce** | I tbs chopped chives or spring onions |
| 2 oz/50g plain flour | |
| I ½ oz/40g butter | |
| I pt/600ml chicken stock | |

*Pancakes*
1. Sieve flour into mixing bowl, make a well in centre and add eggs, milk and water.
2. Mix to a smooth paste with a wooden spoon or small hand whisk. Leave for 30 minutes.
3. Spray a little oil on a non-stick frying pan, heat pan to very hot and turn to medium heat.
4. Pour about 2 tbs batter into pan and tip to allow mixture to coat pan. Cook for 30 seconds.
5. Free edges with palette knife then toss or turn pancake to cook other side.
6. Slide pancake on to warm plate, over pan of hot water, cover with lid and repeat.

*Sauce*
1. Melt butter in small pan over low heat, add flour, stirring well, cook for I minute.
2. Take pan off heat and gradually add stock, stirring continuously.
3. Return to the heat, stir until sauce thickens, simmer for 5 minutes and season.

*Assembling Pancakes*
1. Place slice of gammon and some chicken or turkey on one half of pancake.
2. Add sprinkling of cheese, mixed herbs or stuffing.
3. Fold other half of pancake over the top.
4. Repeat with other pancakes, placing them in oven-proof dish.
5. Pour over freshly prepared sauce, sprinkle with cheese and bake in oven.
6. Remove from oven and sprinkle with finely chopped chives or spring onions.
7. Serve with rice mixed with peas and corn and a green side salad with cherry tomatoes and a French dressing.

*Tim Morgan, Bon Accord, Aberdeen*

# Oriental Duck Breast

Serves: 4

4 duck breasts, skinned and boned

2 tsp vegetable oil

I large onion, sliced

2 red peppers, cut into thin strips

I yellow pepper, cut into thin strips

2 tsp caster sugar

3 pinches chilli powder

sea salt and pepper

8 oz/250g baby spinach

chives, chopped into 2"/5cm lengths

*Sauce*

I tbs vegetable oil

2 garlic cloves, crushed

juice of I lemon,

4 tbs clear honey

3 tbs dark soy sauce

1. Heat griddle pan and add duck. Cook on medium heat for 5-10 minutes each side, depending on size and if rare or well done is required.
2. Heat oil in a small pan, add garlic and cook until softened. Add lemon juice, honey and soy sauce. Stir well and keep warm.
3. Heat oil in wok or large saucepan, add onion and peppers and stir fry for 5 minutes.
4. Add sugar, chilli powder, seasoning and spinach.
5. Mix well and cook for approximately 2 minutes or until spinach begins to wilt.
6. Remove duck to a carving board and allow to rest for a few minutes. Slice thinly.
7. Divide spinach mixture between 4 plates and arrange sliced duck on top.
8. Pour sauce over duck and garnish with chives.

*Jennifer Macleod, Buccleuch & Greyfriars*

# Spicy Duck Breast with Orange Glaze

Pre-heat oven to: 180°C/350°F/Gas4     Time in oven: 15 minutes     Serves: 4

| | |
|---|---|
| 1 tbs coarse sea salt | **Glaze** |
| 2 tsp freshly ground black pepper | zest of 1 orange |
| 3 tsp ground cinnamon | 1/4 pt/150ml fresh orange juice |
| olive oil | 2 tbs runny honey |
| 4 duck breasts | |

1. Mix sea salt, pepper and cinnamon together, add a little olive oil and rub all over duck breasts.
2. Over a high heat, in a frying pan, sear duck breasts, skin side down only, until skin is golden and crispy. Transfer to a roasting dish.
3. Place ingredients for glaze in saucepan. Stir off the heat.
4. Brush a little of the glaze over the duck, turn duck skin side up and roast, brushing skin with more glaze half way through.
5. Towards end of cooking time, boil remaining glaze until it reduces and becomes syrupy.
6. Leave duck to rest for 5 minutes after removing from oven, pour glaze over before serving.
7. Serve with sweet potato mash and green salad.

*Alison MacAskill, Smithton-Culloden*

# Turkey Steaks in Marsala

Pre-heat oven to: 180°C/350°F/Gas4     Time in oven: 10-15 minutes in total     Serves: 4

| | |
|---|---|
| 4 turkey breasts | 4 oz/110g sliced mushrooms, thinly sliced |
| salt and pepper | 1 tbs lemon juice |
| flour for coating | 2 tbs Parmesan cheese, grated |
| 3 oz/75g butter | 6 tbs Marsala wine |
| 1 tbs olive oil | 2 tbs chicken stock |

1. Roll meat thinly. Coat in seasoned flour.
2. Melt 1 1/2 oz/35g butter and oil and fry turkey until golden brown.
3. Put turkey in flat dish in oven.
4. Add 1 oz/25g butter to pan and fry mushrooms until brown. Sprinkle with lemon juice.
5. Using slotted spoon, lift out and place on turkey.
6. Sprinkle Parmesan cheese on top and place in oven for a few minutes until cheese melts.
7. Pour wine into pan and reduce by half. Add stock and 1/2 oz/10g butter and pour over turkey.
8. Return to oven for a few minutes until sauce bubbles.

*Flora Macdonald, Partick, Glasgow*

# Creamy Almond Turkey

Pre-heat oven to: 180°C/350°F/Gas4     Time in oven: 30 minutes     Serves: 4

4 turkey fillets

1 oz/25g butter

2 tsp plain flour

salt and pepper

$^1/_2$ pt/300ml chicken stock

2 tsp tomato purée

1 oz/25g ground almonds

salt and black pepper

1 oz/25g flaked almonds

3$^1/_2$ floz/100ml single cream

1. Fry fillets in butter in oven-proof casserole dish for 2-3 minutes each side until lightly coloured. Remove turkey fillets from casserole dish.
2. Add flour and seasoning and mix.
3. Gradually stir in stock, stirring until smooth. Bring to the boil and simmer for 2 minutes.
4. Stir in tomato purée, ground almonds, salt and pepper and mix well.
5. Return turkey fillets to casserole dish. Cover and bake in oven for 30 minutes.
6. Place flaked almonds in a heated, ungreased frying pan. Shake over heat until almonds are light brown all over.
7. Add cream to cooked turkey and stir.
8. Sprinkle with browned almonds and serve at once.
9. Serve with green pasta and spinach or broccoli.

*Morag Macleod, Perth*

# Turkey with Mushroom and Coriander

Serves 4

2 tbs vegetable oil

1 large onion, chopped

2 cloves garlic, crushed

1 carrot, diced

1$^1/_2$ lbs/700g turkey breast, diced

2 tsp ground coriander

9 floz/295g can condensed cream of mushroom soup

8 oz/225g mushrooms, sliced

ground black pepper

1. Heat oil in pan and sauté onions, garlic and carrot for 5 minutes.
2. Add turkey and brown over a gentle heat.
3. Stir in coriander and mushroom soup. Simmer for 20 minutes, stirring occasionally.
4. Add mushrooms and simmer for a further 20-30 minutes.
5. Just before serving, add ground black pepper to taste.

*Note: The vegetables produce their own liquid, making it unnecessary to dilute the soup.*

*Christine Mackenzie, SOS, Glasgow*

## Casserole of Leg of Lamb

Pre-heat oven to: 180°C/350°F/Gas4      Time in oven: 2 hours      Serves: 4-6

| | |
|---|---|
| 1 leg of lamb | 2 tbs mixed herbs |
| 2 cloves garlic, crushed | 2 tbs tomato purée |
| 2 carrots | 3 lamb stock cubes |

1. Wash leg of lamb, dry with kitchen towel and place in casserole dish.
2. Add garlic, sliced carrots, herbs, tomato purée and crumbled stock cubes.
3. Pour on 1¹/₂ pt/850ml boiling water.
4. Cook in oven until tender.
5. Serve sliced, with potatoes, broccoli, peas and mint sauce.

*Margaret McDonald, Hilton, Fearn*

## Lamb and Pine Nut Pilaf

Serves: 4

| | |
|---|---|
| 1¹/₂ tbs olive oil | 1 oz/25g sultanas |
| 14 oz/400g lean lamb fillet, leg or neck | 1 oz/25g dried apricots, chopped |
| 2 red onions, finely chopped | ¹/₂ tbs fresh parsley, chopped |
| 1 yellow pepper, finely chopped | ¹/₂ tbs fresh mint, chopped |
| 8 oz/225g long grain rice | 18 floz/550ml lamb stock |
| ¹/₂ tsp cumin | 3¹/₂ floz/100ml low fat natural bio yoghurt |
| ¹/₂ tsp coriander | good handful of fresh coriander |
| ¹/₂ tsp cinnamon | ³/₄ oz/20g pine nuts, toasted |
| salt and black pepper | |

1. Cut off any fat from meat and cut into small cubes.
2. Heat half oil in large lidded non-stick frying pan and sauté lamb over low heat, turning once or twice until browned.
3. Remove with slotted spoon and set aside.
4. Add remainder of oil to pan with onions and pepper. Sauté over medium heat for 8 minutes, or until softened and turning golden.
5. Add rice, spices and seasoning and stir for 1 minute. Return lamb to pan.
6. Stir in dried fruits, parsley, mint and stock. Bring to the boil.
7. Reduce heat, cover and simmer for 30 minutes, or until lamb and rice are tender and liquid has been absorbed.
8. Stir in yoghurt and coriander. Sprinkle pine nuts on top and serve.

*Margaret Emslie, Free North, Inverness*

# Colonial Goose

*This is a traditional New Zealand dish. You don't have to bone the leg yourself - maybe a friendly butcher would do it for you. If not, just split the leg open, remove the bone, 'butterfly' the leg, place the stuffing down the middle and roll the leg up, securing it with cocktail sticks.*

Pre-heat oven to: 180°C/350°F/Gas4  Time in oven: 25 mins per 1 lb/450g   Serves: 8-12

**4-5 lb/1.8-2.25kg leg of lamb**

**Stuffing**
**1 oz/25g butter**
**1 tbs runny honey**
**4 oz/110g dried apricots**
**2 oz/50g chopped onion**
**4 oz/110g white breadcrumbs**
**1/4 tsp dried thyme**
**1 egg, beaten**
**1/4 tsp salt**
**freshly ground black pepper**

**Marinade**
**1 large carrot, sliced**
**1/2 onion, sliced**
**1 bay leaf**
**3 parsley stalks**
**1/4 pt/150ml red wine**

1. Using a very sharp knife, bone leg. Work meat away from bone, being careful not to puncture skin.
2. Whizz stuffing ingredients in a food processor.
3. Spoon stuffing into leg cavity. Don't overfill leg, or stuffing will ooze out during cooking.
4. Sew up top and bottom with a trussing needle and fine string.
5. Place filled joint in large polythene bag in large bowl.
6. Add marinade ingredients to bag and leave in fridge for up to 6 hours, turning meat occasionally.
7. Remove from marinade and place in roasting tin in oven. If meat starts to over-brown, cover with foil.
8. To make gravy, add 2-3 tbs marinade to skimmed meat juices. Add a little water and thicken with 1 tsp cornflour mixed with 2 tbs water.
9. Bring to the boil and adjust seasoning.

*Hilary Morrison, Cross, Ness, Lewis*

# Apple Orchard Pork Chops

Serves: 6

| | |
|---|---|
| 2 tsp oil | 2 oz/50g dried currants or raisins |
| I lb/450g thick-cut, boneless pork chops | 2 unpeeled apples, cored and sliced |
| salt and freshly ground pepper | 2 oz/50g sliced spring onions |
| 14 floz/400ml apple juice | 4 tsp cornflour |
| 2 ½ tbs whole grain mustard | 2 ½ floz/75ml water |

1. Heat oil in large non-stick frying pan over medium-high heat.
2. Brown chops, about 2 minutes per side, and season with salt and pepper.
3. Combine apple juice and mustard in small bowl.
4. When chops have browned on both sides, pour over juice mixture.
5. Cover pan, reduce heat, cook chops for 4 minutes.
6. Add currants or raisins, apples and onions. Cover and cook for 5 more minutes.
7. Remove chops to serving platter and cover with foil to keep warm. Reserve cooking liquid.
8. Combine cornflour with water in small bowl and whisk into cooking liquid in pan. Stir until thickened and allow to simmer for 1-2 minutes.
9. Pour sauce and apples over chops and serve.

*Christine Griebel, St Vincent St/Milton, Glasgow*

# Glazed Gammon

Pre-heat oven to: 220°C/425°F/Gas7          Time in oven: 30 minutes          Serves: 15-20

| | |
|---|---|
| 4 lb/1.8kg gammon joint, boned | 12 clementines |
| I ¼ pt/700ml cider | I oz/25g butter |
| 8 oz/225g apricot jam | fresh herbs |
| 2 tbs curry powder | |

1. Soak joint in water for 2-3 hours or overnight. Drain and place in fresh water in large pan.
2. Bring to the boil, simmer for 30 minutes, drain off water and return joint to pan.
3. Pour on cider and sufficient water to cover. Bring to the boil, cover and simmer for 1 hour.
4. Drain, cool slightly, cut away rind while warm and score diagonal pattern on fat with knife.
5. Mix jam and curry powder, warm through with 1-2 tbs water and spread generously over gammon.
6. Roast joint for 30 minutes, re-glazing occasionally.
7. Thoroughly peel clementines and dot with butter. Bake in oven for 10 minutes. Allow to cool or serve hot.
8. Serve joint with clementines and garnish with fresh herbs.

*Anna Stewart, Dowanvale, Glasgow*

# Creamy Mustard Pork

Serves: 2

12 oz/350g pork fillet, thinly sliced
I tbs olive oil
I large onion
I garlic clove, crushed
4 oz/110g button mushrooms, sliced

3 ¹/₂ floz/100ml crème fraîche
I large tbs wholegrain mustard
good handful fresh basil

1. Fry pork in olive oil for 2 minutes on high heat.
2. Toss in onion, garlic and mushrooms and cook for 4-5 minutes.
3. Stir in crème fraîche and mustard and tear in basil.
4. As soon as crème fraîche has gone runny, remove pan from heat.
5. Serve with rice and vegetables.

*Jessie Murray, Cross, Ness, Lewis*

# Tower of Pork and White Fruit Pudding
# with a Calvados and Chive Cream

Serves: 1

I tbs olive oil
6 oz/175g pork medallions
4 oz/110g white fruit pudding
¹/₂ apple
2 oz/50g butter

¹/₄ pt/150ml double cream
2 floz/50ml Calvados
¹/₄ oz/10g fresh chives, chopped
salt and pepper
¹/₂ oz/10g sugar
¹/₂ lime
¹/₂ oz/10g watercress

1. Heat olive oil and pan-fry medallions of pork for 4-6 minutes.
2. Grill white fruit pudding for 2-3 minutes.
3. Dice half apple and pan-fry with butter until soft.
4. Add cream, Calvados and chives and reduce by half.
5. Add seasoning and sugar to your own taste.
6. Build tower of pork and fruit pudding in centre of plate.
7. Pour over Calvados sauce and serve with lime and watercress.

*Iain Graham, Point, Lewis*

# Maple Glazed Pork Tenderloin

Pre-heat oven to: 200°C/400°F/Gas6.    Time in oven: 35 minutes    Serves: 2

12 oz/350g pork tenderloin  
salt and black pepper, freshly ground  
1 tbs vegetable oil

3 tbs maple syrup  
4 tsp Dijon mustard  
2 tsp cider vinegar  
2 tsp soy sauce  
2 tbs minced shallot  
5 floz/150ml chicken stock

1. Lightly sprinkle pork with salt and pepper.
2. Heat oil in large frying pan over medium heat.
3. Add pork, brown on all sides and remove from pan.
4. In a bowl mix syrup, mustard, vinegar, soy sauce, shallot, salt and pepper.
5. Brush pork with extra maple syrup and place in oven-proof dish.
6. Add all other ingredients.
7. Place in oven and cook until tender.

*Catriona MacKay, Cross, Ness, Lewis*

# Pork Apricot à la Crème

Serves: 4

1 pork fillet, cut in strips  
2 tbs flour  
salt and pepper  
2 small onions, chopped  
2 oz/50g butter

2 oz/50g mushrooms, chopped  
1 bay leaf  
1 teacup Shloer grape juice or white wine  
grated rind of 1 small orange, optional  
1 small can apricots, drained  
2 tbs double cream

1. Dip pork strips in seasoned flour.
2. Fry onions in butter and add pork.
3. Add mushrooms, bay leaf and grape juice or wine.
4. Place lid on pan and simmer for 20 minutes.
5. When cooked, add orange rind and chopped apricots.
6. Cool slightly and stir in double cream.
7. Serve on a bed of rice.

*Flora Macleod, Dumbarton*

# Pork Spare Ribs

Pre-heat oven to: 100°C/200°F/Gas ¹/₂          Time in oven: 1 hour          Serves: 2

| | |
|---|---|
| 16 spare ribs | 2 tbs soy sauce |
| 4 floz/125ml vinegar | 2 tbs demerara sugar |
| | 1 tbs honey |
| | 2 cloves garlic |
| | 1 small onion, chopped |
| | 7 floz/200ml tomato ketchup |
| | 2 heaped tsp whole-grain mustard |
| | 1 tbs vinegar |
| | 1 tsp mixed spice |

1. Place ribs in pan and cover with boiling water. Add vinegar, boil for 15 minutes and drain.
2. Mix all other ingredients together.
3. Add ribs, coat well and soak overnight.
4. Cook in oven-proof dish.
5. Serve with side salad and crusty bread.

*Note: Serves 2 as a main course and 4 as a starter.*

*P. Nicholson, North Uist, Grimsay and Berneray*

# Fricassee of Pork with Potato and Mushroom

Pre-heat oven to 180°C/350°F/Gas4          Time in oven: 1-1¹/₂ hours          Serves: 4

| | |
|---|---|
| 1 tsp olive oil | 1 lb/450g potatoes, peeled and cubed |
| 1 medium onion, peeled and chopped | 10 medium mushrooms, washed and sliced |
| 1 lb/450g lean stewing pork, cubed | 12 floz/350ml dry white wine |
| 1 tbs plain flour | 14 floz/400ml chicken stock |
| salt and pepper | 1 tbs cranberry jelly |
| | 3 ¹/₂ floz/100ml double cream |
| | parsley to garnish |

1. Heat oil in pan. Add onion and fry until golden.
2. Add pork, fry until browned, stir in flour and season.
3. Add potato, mushroom, wine and stock and bring to the boil.
4. Transfer to casserole, cover and cook in oven until meat is tender.
5. Remove casserole from oven, stir in cranberry jelly and gradually add cream.
6. Return to oven, heat through and garnish with parsley.

*Fiona Harris, Burghead*

 **pasta**

## Chicken and Bacon Pasta

Serves: 6

2 tbs olive oil
3 large chicken breasts, thinly sliced
4 rashers smoked bacon, chopped
bunch spring onions, sliced
2 florets broccoli, broken into tiny sprigs
2-3 cloves garlic, crushed

14 oz/400g can chopped tomatoes
6 sun-dried tomatoes in oil, chopped
2 tbs tomato paste
I can flagelot or cannelini beans or chick peas
black pepper, freshly milled
2 heaped tbs crème fraîche
2 tbs Feta cheese, cubed
2 tbs green and black unstuffed olives
12 oz/350g pasta shapes or tagliatelle, cooked
handful fresh basil leaves, torn

1. Add oil to very hot wok or large open pan and stir-fry chicken and bacon for 5 minutes, or until cooked.
2. Add spring onions, broccoli sprigs and garlic and cook for further few minutes.
3. Add chopped tomatoes, sun-dried tomatoes, tomato paste, beans and pepper.
4. Bring to the boil.
5. Stir in crème fraîche, cubed cheese and olives.
6. Add cooked pasta shapes or tagliatelle.
7. Place in large serving bowl and sprinkle basil over top.
8. Serve with crisp green salad.

*Catherine Bowe, Lochgilphead*

# Creamy Mushroom Pasta

Serves: 4

12 oz/350g pasta
1 tbs olive oil
3 oz/75g butter
2 shallots, chopped finely

2 cloves garlic, crushed
1 tbs parsley, freshly chopped
7 oz/200g mushrooms, sliced
3 1/2 floz/100ml white wine
1 pt/600ml double cream

1. Cook pasta as instructed on packet.
2. Melt olive oil and butter in frying pan and fry shallots until lightly coloured.
3. Add garlic, parsley and mushrooms and mix well.
4. Cook thoroughly but gently until almost brown.
5. Add wine and simmer gently until wine has almost disappeared. Add cream and mix thoroughly.
6. Drain cooked pasta, return to pan, drizzle with olive oil, season and stir well.
7. Add a little sauce to coat pasta. Transfer to large heated serving bowl. Top with remainder of sauce.
8. Serve with crusty garlic bread and green salad.

*Mary Macmillan, Dowanvale, Glasgow*

# Pasta and Meatball Bake

Pre-heat oven to: 200°C/400°F/Gas6     Time in oven: 30 mins     Serves: 4

1 lb/450g lean minced beef
2 oz/50g canned sweetcorn, drained
2 tbs tomato ketchup
2 tbs oil

8 oz/225g penne pasta, cooked
1 lb/450g jar tomato pasta sauce
1/2 pt/300ml boiling water
2 oz/50g Cheddar cheese, grated

1. In a large bowl, mix mince with sweetcorn and ketchup.
2. Shape mixture into 16 meatballs and fry in oil until browned.
3. Place pasta in large oven-proof dish and arrange meatballs evenly over top.
4. Pour over jar of pasta sauce, mixed with boiling water, making sure that all pasta is covered.
5. Scatter with grated cheese, cook in oven until meat is browned and cheese is bubbling.
6. Serve with garlic bread and green salad.

*Mairi MacRae, Sleat & Strath, Skye*

**pasta**

# Tomato and Prawn Pasta Bake

Pre-heat oven to: 180°C/350°F/Gas4      Time in oven: 10-15 minutes      Serves: 6

| | |
|---|---|
| 1 lb 2 oz/500g spiral pasta | 2 tbs chopped fresh oregano |
| 2 tbs olive oil | 2 x 14 oz/400g cans tomatoes |
| 2 ½ oz/60g butter | 3 tbs dry sherry |
| 2 leeks, sliced | 2lb 3 oz/1kg uncooked prawns, shelled & |
| 4 cloves garlic, crushed | chopped |
| 1 tsp chilli powder | 7 oz/200g cheese, crumbled |

1. Cook pasta as instructed on packet.
2. Heat oil in pan with butter and add leeks, garlic and chilli. Cook, stirring until leeks are soft, then add oregano.
3. Add undrained tomatoes, sherry and prawns and bring to the boil. Simmer for 1 minute.
4. Spoon pasta into greased oven-proof dish. Top with prawn mixture.
5. Sprinkle with cheese. Just before serving bake in oven until cheese is browned and pasta heated through. Serve immediately.

*Nan MacAulay, Keose, Lewis*

# Tomato and Mascarpone Pasta

Serves: 4

| | |
|---|---|
| 1 onion | 3 tbs Mascarpone cheese |
| 2 garlic cloves, crushed | 12 oz/350g pasta |
| 1 tbs tomato purée | |
| ½ tsp sugar | |
| 1 tbs fresh basil, chopped | |
| 14 oz/400g can tomatoes | |
| 1 tsp balsamic vinegar | |

1. Cook pasta according to packet instructions.
2. Sauté onion and garlic for few minutes.
3. Add other ingredients except cheese and pasta. Cook over medium heat for approximately 10 minutes.
4. Blend if desired. Stir in cheese.
5. Add to drained pasta and serve.

*Rachel Rae, Dingwall*

# Creamy Pasta with Chicken and Spring Vegetables

Pre-heat oven to: 220°C/425°F/Gas7     Time in oven: 10-12 minutes     Serves: 6

| | |
|---|---|
| 8 oz/225g thin fresh asparagus | 1/4 tsp salt |
| I large red bell pepper, sliced thinly | 1/4 tsp coarsely ground black pepper |
| 8 oz/225g mushrooms, sliced | 2 tbs fresh basil leaves, snipped or I tsp dried basil |
| 3-4 chicken breasts, cooked and diced | 8 oz/225g uncooked rigatoni |
| 2 tbs olive oil | 6 floz/175ml whipping cream |
| 3 garlic cloves, crushed | 2 oz/50g fresh Parmesan cheese, grated |

1. Snap off and discard tough ends of asparagus. Cut into 1 1/2"/4cm pieces and place in large bowl.
2. Add pepper, mushrooms and chicken.
3. Add olive oil and mix lightly. Season chicken and vegetables with garlic, salt and pepper.
4. Pour into shallow casserole dish or baking sheet and bake until vegetables are tender.
5. Prepare pasta according to package directions.
6. In small pan simmer whipping cream for 6-8 minutes over medium-low heat to thicken slightly, stirring constantly with whisk.
7. Drain pasta and transfer to large bowl.
8. Add chicken and vegetables, heated cream and basil, mixing lightly.
9. Add half Parmesan cheese into pasta mixture, mix lightly and spoon on to serving plates.
10. Sprinkle with additional black pepper and remaining grated cheese.

*Janette Macrae, Portree*

# Red Pepper and Chilli Pasta

Pre-heat oven to: 220°C/425°F/Gas7     Time in oven: I hour     Serves: 4

| | |
|---|---|
| 8 oz/225g pasta | 2 red chillies |
| 2 large red peppers | freshly ground black pepper |
| 2 floz/50ml sun-dried tomatoes in oil | salt |
| 4 floz/125ml olive oil | I tbs fresh thyme |
| 2 garlic cloves | Parmesan cheese, freshly grated |

1. Cook pasta according to instructions on packet.
2. Roast peppers in oven until skin is black.
3. Place in bowl and cover with cling film. When cool remove black skin and discard.
4. De-seed peppers and cut up flesh. Place in blender with remaining ingredients apart from cheese.
5. Place hot pasta in serving dish, pour over cold pepper mixture, and toss.
6. Sprinkle with freshly grated Parmesan cheese and serve immediately.

*Marilyn McDonald, Cumbernauld*

# desserts

## Alison's Coffee and Amaretto Trifle

Serves: 8

14 floz/400ml strong coffee

3 floz/75ml DiSaronno or amaretto liqueur

1 lb/450g tub Mascarpone cheese

1 lb/450g fresh custard

9 oz/250g Italian sponge biscuits

9 oz/250g raspberries

1 tbs chocolate coffee beans

1 tbs flaked almonds

1. Mix coffee and amaretto liqueur in wide bowl.
2. Beat mascarpone and custard with blender.
3. Dip one third of sponge biscuits in coffee mixture until soft but not soggy and use to line base of dish. Drizzle over more coffee mixture.
4. Reserve some raspberries for decoration. Sprinkle over one third of raspberries.
5. Smooth over one third of mascarpone mixture.
6. Repeat layers twice.
7. Chill overnight or for at least 2 hours.
8. Decorate with chocolate coffee beans, almonds or raspberries.

*Note: Trifle sponge cakes can be used instead of Italian sponge biscuits.*

*Emma Lipp, Bon Accord, Aberdeen*

## Banana and Flake Trifle

Serves: 6

4 oz/110g plain, white or milk chocolate

14 oz/400g tub or home-made custard

1/2 pt/300ml double cream, softly whipped

4 small bananas

2 tsp lemon juice

4 large Cadbury's Flakes, roughly chopped

1. Melt chocolate in bowl set over pan of simmering water.
2. Stir custard into half of melted chocolate and set aside.
3. Beat a little cream into remaining melted chocolate and carefully fold in remaining cream.
4. Peel and slice bananas. Toss in lemon juice to prevent browning.
5. Place Flakes in a serving dish, reserving some for decoration.
6. Cover with half of banana slices, then spoon over half of chocolate custard.
7. Cover with remaining banana slices and chocolate custard.
8. Spoon chocolate cream over in large blobs. Sprinkle with reserved flakes.

*Wilma Nicolson, Bon Accord, Aberdeen*

# Diana's Chocolate Mousse

Serves: 6-8

| | |
|---|---|
| I large can evaporated milk | I tbs Camp coffee |
| $^1/2$ oz/I0g gelatine | 2 tbs cocoa |
| 2 tbs boiling water | 2 tbs drinking chocolate |
| 2 tbs caster sugar | $^1/2$ pt/300ml double cream |
| | I Cadbury's Flake |

1. Chill milk in fridge or freezer.
2. Whisk milk with electric mixer until very stiff.
3. Dissolve gelatine in boiling water in bowl and place in pan of simmering water.
4. Add sugar to gelatine and stir until dissolved.
5. Add coffee, cocoa and drinking chocolate, stirring well. If necessary, add some more boiling water.
6. When cooled but not set, fold gently into beaten milk and mix thoroughly.
7. Pour into serving dish or individual dishes and allow to set in fridge.
8. Top with whipped double cream and then Flake broken and sprinkled on top.

*Catherine Bowe, Lochgilphead*

# Iced Ginger Meringue

Pre-heat oven to: 100°C/200°F/Gas $^1/2$     Time in oven: $2^1/2$-3 hours     Serves: 4-6

| | |
|---|---|
| 2 egg whites | $^1/2$ pt/300ml plain unsweetened yoghurt |
| $3^1/2$ oz/90g soft light brown sugar | 4 tbs double cream |
| $^1/2$ tsp ground ginger | lemon rind |
| | 2 tsp lemon juice |

1. Whisk egg whites until stiff and whisk in half sugar until mixture is stiff and glossy.
2. Mix remaining sugar with ground ginger and fold into egg whites.
3. Spoon mixture in mounds on to non-stick silicone paper.
4. Bake meringues until they are dry.
5. Whip together yoghurt and cream and beat in lemon rind and juice.
6. Break cooled meringues into chunks and stir into mixture.
7. Put mixture into a I lb/450g loaf tin lined with foil, cover with foil and freeze for 3 hours.
8. Turn meringue loaf on to serving dish and leave in fridge for 30 minutes before serving.

*Note: Greek yoghurt is best.*

*Anne Mitchell, Perth*

# Mixed Summer Salad

Serves: 8-10

¹/4 pt/150ml dry white wine or fresh orange juice
juice of 1 large orange
¹/4 pt/150ml water
3 oz/75g caster sugar

8 oz/225g strawberries
1 small melon
2 large peaches
2 tsp chopped mint, optional

1. Put wine, orange juice, water and sugar in a pan.
2. Heat gently until sugar dissolves.
3. Bring to the boil and boil rapidly for 5 minutes or until syrupy.
4. Leave to cool.
5. Pour over chopped and prepared fruit.
6. Place in fridge for a few hours to allow flavours to mix and develop.
7. Serve with chopped mint and cream.

*Note: Use any fruit in season: e.g. oranges, bananas, grapes, apples.*

*Dina Begg, Lybster*

# "Never Fail" Cheesecake

Serves: 6

**Base**
4 oz/110g digestive biscuits
2 oz/50g margarine, melted

**Filling**
1 packet orange jelly, or any flavour
¹/4 pt/150ml double cream
7 oz/200g Philadelphia light cheese
4 oz/110g icing sugar, sifted
¹/2 tsp vanilla essence
¹/4 pt/150ml soured cream
1 small can mandarin orange segments

1. Crush biscuits and mix with melted margarine.
2. Press into a greased 8"/20cm loose-based tin.
3. Mix jelly in ¹/4 pt boiling water and leave to cool.
4. Lightly whip double cream.
5. In second bowl mix cheese, sugar and vanilla essence.
6. Add mixture to whipped double cream and mix well.
7. Mix in soured cream, add jelly and whip.
8. Pour on to biscuit base and leave to set in fridge overnight.
9. Top with mandarin oranges or appropriate fruit just before serving.

*Margaret Grant, Falkirk*

# Vanilla Cream Terrine

Serves: 6

| | |
|---|---|
| 15 floz/425ml whipping cream | 2 tsp vanilla extract |
| 1 sachet gelatine powder | 15 floz/425ml natural yoghurt |
| 3 oz/75g caster sugar | 18 oz/500g soft red berries |

1. Place 3 tbs cream in a small bowl and add gelatine.
2. Leave for 5-10 minutes.
3. Put remaining cream and sugar in a saucepan and heat gently until sugar dissolves.
4. Add gelatine mixture and heat until dissolved. Do not allow to boil.
5. In a bowl, stir vanilla and yoghurt together, pour on cream mixture through a sieve and mix thoroughly.
6. Pour in to a 10" x 3"/25.5cm x 7.5cm plastic box and chill.
7. Turn out on to a serving tray, decorate with mixed red berries and serve with a coulis.

*Coulis*

| | |
|---|---|
| 18 oz/500g soft red berries | 3 oz/75g caster sugar |

1. Mix together and soak for 30 minutes.
2. Sieve through a fine mesh strainer and serve.

*Note: Other fruits can be used.*

*Mary Morrison, Scalpay*

# Raspberry Sponge

Pre-heat oven to: 180°C/350°F/Gas4    Time in oven: 35 minutes    Serves: 10-12

| | |
|---|---|
| 6 oz/175g butter, soft | 10 oz/275g raspberries |
| 6 oz/175g soft brown sugar | icing sugar |
| 3 eggs | |
| 6 oz/175g S.R. flour | |
| 6 oz/175g ground almonds | |
| 1 tsp cinnamon | |
| 2 tbs milk | |

1. Line the base of a 9"/23cm spring form cake tin with non-stick baking paper.
2. Place all ingredients except raspberries and icing sugar in a processor.
3. Blend until smooth or mix thoroughly by hand.
4. Spread half the mixture in base of tin.
5. Spoon over raspberries.
6. Cover with remaining cake mix.
7. Bake in oven until firm to the touch.
8. Cool for 10 minutes and remove from tin.
9. Dust with icing sugar.
10. Serve warm with ice cream and raspberry coulis, see recipe above.

*Nan Ferguson, Ness, Lewis*

# "Popping Out" Apple Pie

Pre-heat oven to: 200°C/400°F/Gas6 Time in oven: I hour Serves: 12

I large or 2 medium cooking apples
2-3 tbs lemon juice
I tsp vanilla essence
3 eggs
4 oz/110g sugar
pinch of salt

4 oz/110g plain flour
I tsp baking powder
6 tbs oil
2 oz/50g butter
icing sugar

1. Peel, core and slice apples and sprinkle with lemon juice and vanilla essence.
2. In a mixing bowl beat together eggs, sugar and salt.
3. Gradually add flour and baking powder. Add oil quickly and mix thoroughly.
4. Pour batter into a greased 8"/20cm hinged baking tin and spread pieces of apple evenly on top.
5. Bake in middle of oven.
6. Pastry should be popping out between pieces of apple and be golden brown in colour.
7. Take out of oven, brush with melted butter and sprinkle with icing sugar.
8. Remove from tin when cold.

*I. L. Slidders, St. Peter's, Dundee*

# Apple Cake with Hot Caramel Sauce

Pre-heat oven to: 180°C/350°F/Gas4 Time in oven: 50-60 mins Serves: 10-12

14 oz/400g granulated sugar
2 eggs
8 floz/250ml vegetable oil
10 oz/275g S.R. flour
2 large cooking apples, diced
4 oz/110g chopped walnuts
$3/4$ tsp cinnamon

*Hot Caramel Sauce*
6 oz/175g light brown sugar
4 oz/110g butter
I tsp vanilla essence
4 floz/125ml evaporated milk

1. Combine cake ingredients in a large bowl and mix well.
2. Pour into a greased 9" x 13"/23cm x 32.5cm oven-proof dish and bake in oven.
3. Make caramel sauce by melting butter with brown sugar in a sauce pan over medium heat. Bring to the boil and stir constantly with a hand whisk.
4. Remove from heat and add vanilla essence and evaporated milk. Whisk until well blended.
5. When cake is cooked, prick warm cake with skewer and pour sauce over letting it soak into the cake.

*Christine Griebel, St Vincent Street/Milton, Glasgow*

# Miracle Pudding

Pre-heat oven to: 190°C/375°F/Gas5    Time in oven: 1 hour    Serves: 8

**Base**
5 oz/150g margarine
10 oz/275g S.R. flour
4 tsp baking powder
4 tsp sugar
8 oz/225g sultanas
1 teacup milk

**Sauce**
4 teacups boiling water
8 oz/225g soft brown sugar
3 oz/75g margarine

1. Rub margarine into flour until mixture resembles fine breadcrumbs.
2. Add all other base ingredients and stir together with milk.
3. Place in a 4"/10cm deep, 9"/23cm diameter oven-proof dish.
4. Melt together sauce ingredients and pour over cake mixture.
5. Bake in oven. Serve hot with whipped cream.

*C Ross, Lochcarron*

# South African Apple Tart

Pre-heat oven to: 170°C/325°F/Gas3    Time in oven: 45 minutes    Serves: 6-8

1 lb/450g cooking apples
4 oz/110g margarine
2 tbs caster sugar
2 tbs oil
1 small tsp vanilla
1 egg

8 oz/225g plain flour
2 level tsp baking powder
2 oz/50g sultanas
1 heaped tsp spice

1. Wash, quarter, peel, core and slice apples. Place in salted water and set aside.
2. Cream together margarine, sugar, oil and vanilla.
3. Beat in egg and add sifted flour and baking powder. This forms dough rather than pastry.
4. Press three quarters of dough into a greased 8"/20cm pie dish.
5. Strain apples, mix with sultanas and spice and place over dough in pie dish.
6. Use a coarse grater to grate remaining dough over apple mix.
7. Bake in oven until golden brown.

*Christine Davidson, Watten*

# Whisky and Orange Pancakes

Pre-heat oven to: 170°C/325°F/Gas3         Time in oven: 10 minutes         Makes: 12

**Pancake batter**

4 oz/110g plain flour

$^3/_4$ tsp salt

2 eggs

$^1/_2$ pt/300ml milk

2 tbs oil

a little butter for frying

**Sauce**

3 oz/75g butter

4 oz/110g caster sugar

$^1/_4$ pt/150ml freshly squeezed orange juice

grated zest of 1 large orange

grated zest and juice of 2 lemons

3 tbs whisky

*Pancakes*
1. Sift flour and salt into large bowl.
2. Make well in centre and break in eggs.
3. Whisk with one hand and gradually pour in milk with the other until batter is smooth and lump-free.
4. Add oil and whisk again.
5. Heat frying pan, not more than 7"/18cm in diameter, and swirl knob of butter to coat the base. Tip out excess melted butter on to saucer and use for next pancake.
6. Pour 2 tbs batter into hot pan, swirl it around evenly and, as soon as it looks golden brown on underneath edge, flip it over and brown on other side.
7. Fold pancake in half and in half again and place in a shallow gratin dish. Repeat until all pancakes are made.

*Sauce*
1. Melt butter, stir in sugar and simmer for 5 minutes.
2. Add orange, lemon juice and zest. Bring to simmering point.
3. Add whisky and simmer for 3 minutes.
4. Pour sauce over pancakes. It will look too much at this stage but fear not - pancakes will soak up and absorb sauce.
5. Place dish in oven for 10 minutes.

*Note: Pancakes can be made in advance. Pour sauce over and immediately reheat in oven for 15 minutes.*

*Annabel Robertson, St. Peter's, Dundee*

# Caramel Queen Pudding

Pre-heat oven to: 170°C/325°F/Gas3     Time in oven: 30 minutes     Serves: 4

3 oz/75g syrup

1/2 oz/10g butter

1/2 pt/300ml milk

2 oz/50g breadcrumbs

1 large egg, separated

1/2 tsp vanilla essence

1 1/2 oz/35g caster sugar

1. Cook syrup and butter in saucepan until a deep golden colour.
2. Add milk and slowly bring to the boil, stirring continuously.
3. Stir in breadcrumbs and leave mixture to cool slightly.
4. Beat in egg yolk and essence and transfer to a 1 pt/600ml greased heat-proof dish.
5. Bake in centre of oven.
6. Whisk egg white until very stiff and fold in sugar.
7. Cover pudding with meringue and return to oven to brown.
8. Leave to cool and serve with cream or ice-cream.

*Peggy Macdonald, Dowanvale*

# Citrus Bread and Butter Pudding

Pre-heat oven to: 180°C/350°F/Gas4     Time in oven: 30 minutes     Serves: 4-6

2 oz/50g softened butter

12 thick slices white bread

4 oz/110g sultanas

1/2 pt/300ml double cream

3/4 pt/450ml milk

juice from 1/2 lemon and 1/2 orange

3 medium eggs

3 oz/75g caster sugar

pinch of nutmeg

icing sugar for dusting

1. Generously butter each slice of bread and cut into triangles.
2. Grease ovenproof dish and line base with layers of bread and sultanas.
3. Whisk together all remaining ingredients, pour over bread and bake until well risen.
4. Sprinkle with icing sugar and serve warm.

*Mary Smith, Point, Lewis*

# Jam Roly Poly

Pre-heat oven to: 180°C/350°F/Gas4    Time in oven: 35-40 minutes    Serves: 4-6

pinch of salt

8 oz/225g S.R. flour

4 oz/110g margarine

2 floz/50ml cold water

4 tbs jam

2 oz/50g margarine

3 oz/75g sugar

6 floz/180ml boiling water

1. Add salt to flour and rub in margarine.
2. Add water to make stiff dough.
3. Roll on floured surface to approximately 8 "x 9¹/₂"/20cm x 24cm and spread with jam.
4. Roll up, seal edges and place in buttered dish.
5. Melt margarine, dissolve sugar in boiling water and mix together.
6. Pour over pudding and bake. Serve with pouring custard.

*Note: Syrup, marmalade or fruit purée may be used instead of jam.*

*Margaret Main, Burghead*

# Lemon Meringue Pie

Pre-heat oven to: 200°C/400°F/Gas6    Time in oven: 30-35 mins in total    Serves: 8-10

*Pastry*

6 oz/175g plain flour

pinch of salt

3 oz/75g margarine

2 tbs cold water

*Filling*

3 egg yolks

1 large can condensed milk

grated rind and juice of 2 lemons

*Meringue*

3 egg whites

6 oz/175g caster sugar

1. Make pastry case for an 8"/20cm diameter flan dish. (See page no 137)
2. Combine egg yolks, condensed milk, lemon juice and rind together.
3. Pour into baked pastry flan case.
4. Make meringue by whisking egg whites together until very thick.
5. Add caster sugar and continue to whisk until meringue is thick again.
6. Pile meringue on top of filling and bake at 180°C/355°F/Gas4 for 15-20minutes or for longer at a lower temperature for a crisper meringue.

*Sallie Bremner, Bon Accord, Aberdeen*

# The Ultimate Sticky Toffee Pudding

Pre-heat oven to: 180°C/350°F/Gas4     Time in oven: 35 minutes     Serves: 8-10

**2 oz/50g margarine**
**5 oz/150g caster sugar**
**5 oz/150g dates, stoned & chopped**
**¼ pt/150ml water**
**½ large can evaporated milk**
**I tsp bicarbonate of soda**
**2 eggs**
**5 oz/150g S.R. flour**

*Toffee Sauce*
**2 oz/50g butter**
**6 oz/175g brown sugar**
**½ large can evaporated milk**

1. Grease a medium-sized oven-proof dish, or ramekin dishes for individual puddings.
2. In a microwave jug, bring to the boil dates, evaporated milk and water.
3. Remove from heat and add bicarbonate of soda. Allow to cool.
4. Beat margarine and caster sugar together.
5. Gradually beat in eggs and flour.
6. Stir in date mixture.
7. Pour into dish(es) and bake for approximately 35 minutes. A shorter time will be required for ramekins. Test with skewer.
8. Place all sauce ingredients into pan and bring to the boil, stirring continuously. Simmer for 2-3 minutes and pour over pudding.
9. Serve with double cream or ice cream.

*Note: This pudding can be made in advance and then reheated in the microwave for a few minutes, but take care not to overheat. Sauce can be served separately if liked.*

*Rena Maclean, Smithton-Culloden*

# easy entertaining

## Parsnip and Satsuma or Clementine Soup

Serves: 4

1 lb/450g parsnip, peeled and cut in chunks
2 onions, quartered
2 cloves garlic, peeled and crushed

juice of 2 satsumas or clementines
¼ level tsp garlic pepper
1 tsp dried parsley
1 organic chicken cube

1. Put all ingredients in pan and cover with water.
2. Simmer until vegetables are just cooked - don't overcook.
3. Cool, liquidize and adjust consistency to taste with more fruit juice if required.
4. Serve with a swirl of cream, if desired.

*Margaret Macleod, Tain*

## Red or Yellow Pepper Soup

Serves: 4

4 tbs olive oil
2 garlic cloves, crushed
6 large peppers, sliced
2 onions

2 pt/1.2litre stock
1 tbs white vinegar
pinch of caster sugar
freshly ground black pepper
3 floz/75ml double cream, optional
parsley to garnish

1. In heavy based pan put olive oil, garlic, peppers and onions. Sauté for 15 minutes.
2. Add stock, vinegar and sugar. Boil for 15 minutes, add black pepper.
3. Cool and liquidize.
4. If creamy consistency desired, add 1-2 tbs cornflour, blended with a little milk.
5. Return to heat, stirring all the time and allow to simmer for 1-2 minutes.
6. Add cream, if desired.
7. Season and garnish with parsley.

*Nina MacLeod, Portmahomack, Inverness*

# Quick Pea Soup

Serves: 4

I tbs oil
4 or 5 rashers smoked streaky bacon
I onion, sliced
I carrot, sliced

II oz/300g can mushy peas
I chicken stock cube
I pt/600ml boiling water

1. Roughly snip bacon and sauté in oil for 2 minutes.
2. Add onion and carrot and stir for further 2 minutes.
3. Add peas and stock cube dissolved in water. Simmer for 20 minutes.
4. Blend and serve with croutons.

*Mary Maguire, Dumfries*

# Tomato, Lentil and Apple Soup

Serves: 6-8

2 tbs vegetable oil
I onion, chopped
2 carrots, chopped
8 oz/225g lentils
2 cooking apples, chopped

2 large cans chopped tomatoes
I pt/600ml vegetable or chicken stock
2 tbs tomato purée
salt and pepper

1. Heat oil and sauté onion and carrots for 5 minutes.
2. Add lentils and apples and cook for 10 minutes.
3. Add tomatoes, stock, tomato purée and seasoning.
4. Bring to the boil and simmer for 45 minutes.
5. Blend, using a hand blender or liquidizer.

*Donna Maciver, Garrabost, Lewis*

# Quick and Tasty Onion Soup

Serves: 2

I large onion
I tbs oil
½ tsp caster sugar

I pt/600ml stock
I dsp semolina, optional

1. Slice onion thinly.
2. Fry gently in oil, until soft. This may take 15 minutes.
3. Sprinkle sugar over and cook a little longer, giving onion a golden colour.
4. Add stock and bring to the boil for 10-15 minutes.
5. For extra body, mix semolina in cold milk or water, pour into soup and stir until soup thickens.

*Elma Mackenzie, Assynt Free/APC*

# Quick Tuna Paté

Serves: 4

7 oz/200g can of tuna in brine, drained

4 oz/110g cream cheese

3 tbs mayonnaise

2 tsp lemon juice

salt and black pepper

I lemon, cut into wedges

1. Place all ingredients, apart from lemon, in food processor.
2. Blend together in short bursts to make smooth mixture.
3. Garnish with lemon wedges.
4. Serve with salad or crusty bread.

*Tina MacLeod, Greyfriars, Inverness*

# Harvest Loaf

Pre-heat oven to: 200°C/400°F/Gas6          Time in oven: 1 1/2 hours          Serves: 4-6

8 oz/225g minced beef

8 oz/225g bacon, chopped finely

I onion, chopped finely

I carrot, grated

I tsp mustard

I oz/25g oatmeal

I egg, beaten

I tbs fresh parsley, chopped

salt and pepper

1. Mix all above ingredients together.
2. Shape into a roll.
3. Wrap in tin foil, place on baking tray and bake in oven.
4. Can be served hot with vegetables or cold with salad.

*Irene Chisholm, Inverasdale*

# Marenco Beef
Pre-heat oven to: 180°C/350°F/Gas4     Time in oven: 40 minutes     Serves: 4

1 tbs olive oil

1 onion, chopped

7 oz/200g mushrooms, sliced

1 lb 4 oz/560g steak mince

1 can Campbell's tomato soup

1 can Campbell's mushroom soup

3 oz/75g Cheddar cheese, grated

1. Heat oil in pan and sauté onions and mushrooms.
2. Add mince and fry, stirring well to break up meat.
3. Drain off any excess fat.
4. Mix two soups together in bowl.
5. Put meat, onions and mushrooms into casserole dish.
6. Pour in soup, stir in grated cheese, cover and bake in oven.
7. Serve with noodles, rice, pasta or mashed potatoes and salad.

*Annie Mckinnon, Scalpay*

# Norwegian Stew
Pre-heat oven to: 180°C/350°F/Gas4     Time in oven: 2$^1$/$_2$ hours     Serves: 4

1 lb/450g stewing steak

1-2 tbs oil

1 stock cube

15 floz/425ml water

1 tbs Worcester sauce

1 tbs flour

4 tbs tomato sauce

2 tbs vinegar

2 tbs brown sugar

1 dsp curry powder

salt and pepper

1. Heat oil in frying pan until very hot. Fry meat until brown.
2. Put all ingredients except steak, stock cube and water in casserole dish and stir.
3. Add stock cube, dissolved in water and meat.
4. Cover and cook in oven.
5. Serve with rice or potatoes.

*Alice Ross, Dornoch*

# Bacon Wrapped Chicken Breasts

Pre-heat oven to: 180°C/350°F/Gas4    Time in oven: 30 minutes    Serves: 4

**4 chicken breasts**
**Roulade soft garlic cheese**
**8 slices bacon**
**oil**

**Sauce**
**I onion**
**2 slices bacon**
**I clove garlic**
**I tbs oil**
**¹/₂ pt/300ml cream**

1. Make slice in top of each chicken breast to form pocket.
2. Fill each pocket with soft cheese and close.
3. Wrap bacon round chicken, place in a greased and covered casserole dish and bake until chicken is cooked and juices run clear.
4. Remove lid 5 minutes before end of cooking to crisp bacon.

*Sauce*
1. Finely chop onion and bacon. Crush garlic.
2. Heat oil in frying pan and sauté garlic.
3. Add bacon and onion. Fry until onion is soft.
4. Pour in cream and simmer for a few minutes.
5. Place cooked chicken on serving dish and pour over sauce.

*Sara A MacLean, Ballantrushual, Lewis*

# Baked Summer Chicken

Pre-heat oven to: 200°C/400°F/Gas6    Time in oven: 35-40 mins in total    Serves: 4

**8 chicken thighs**
**salt and pepper**
**I tbs oil**
**I lb 4 oz/550g baby new potatoes, scrubbed**

**2 lemons, quartered**
**3 tbs clear honey**
**small bunch of fresh tarragon**

1. Heat a large frying pan. Dry-fry chicken thighs, skin-side down, for a few minutes until golden brown and juices run clear.
2. Transfer to large baking dish, reserving juices in pan. Season chicken.
3. Add oil to juices in pan, fry potatoes until lightly browned and add to baking dish.
4. Push lemon wedges between chicken thighs. Bake for 20 minutes.
5. Remove baking dish and drizzle chicken with honey. Return to oven for a further 15-20 minutes until cooked through and golden.
6. Scatter freshly torn tarragon over chicken and new potatoes.
7. Serve with green beans, baby sweet corn and roasted red peppers.

*Fiona Richards, Cumbernauld*

# Chicken and Avocado Wraps

Serves: 4

4 chicken breasts, cut into strips

juice of I lemon

juice of I lime

2 handfuls of mixed salad leaves

I large ripe avocado, peeled and chopped

2 tbs natural or Greek yoghurt

4 flat breads or flour tortillas

1. Marinade chicken strips in lemon and lime juice for at least I hour.
2. Stir-fry and set aside.
3. Mix salad leaves, avocado and yoghurt in bowl. Mix in chicken.
4. Warm tortillas.
5. Arrange chicken and salad in tortillas and serve with cous cous and stir-fried peppers.

*Sarah Lytle, Buccleuch and Greyfriars, Edinburgh*

# Chicken and Courgette Medley

Pre-heat oven to: 180°C/350°F/Gas4    Time in oven: 40-50 minutes    Serves: 6

6 chicken breasts

3 tbs flour

3 tbs olive oil

4 cloves garlic, crushed

I large onion, diced

2 courgettes, cut into I"/2.5cm pieces

2 tomatoes, cut into wedges

2 tsp fresh rosemary, finely chopped

6 floz/175ml chicken stock

salt and pepper

I red and I yellow pepper, sliced

1. Dredge chicken breasts in flour.
2. Heat oil in large frying pan and fry chicken gently until seared and golden brown, turning once.
3. Transfer to large oven-proof dish.
4. Add remaining ingredients, cover with foil and place in oven.

*Connie Thomson, East Kilbride*

# Garlic Mushroom Chicken

Pre-heat oven to: 150°C/300°F/Gas3　　Time in oven: 1-1¹/2 hours　　Serves: 4

oil

4 chicken joints

1 can Campbell's cream of mushroom soup

¹/2 pt/300ml single cream

2 cloves garlic, crushed

salt and pepper

4 oz/110g mushrooms, sliced

paprika

1. Oil chicken joints and place in covered casserole dish. Cook in oven for 1 hour.
2. Mix soup, cream, garlic, salt, pepper and mushrooms in bowl.
3. Remove casserole from oven, add juice from chicken joints to mixture in bowl and stir well.
4. Pour mixture over chicken joints and sprinkle paprika over top.
5. Leave lid off and return to oven for about 30 minutes, until nicely browned.

*Elisabeth Mackay, Bishopbriggs*

# Mexican Chicken

Serves: 2-3

2 small tubs natural yoghurt

2 tbs mayonnaise

2 tbs tomato ketchup

1 tsp garlic granules

¹/2 tsp chilli powder

1 green pepper, cut into strips

1 red pepper, cut into strips

1 onion, chopped

1 small can sweet corn

2 cooked chicken breasts, torn into strips

1. In a saucepan stir together yoghurt, mayonnaise, ketchup and garlic.
2. Add chilli powder, peppers, onions, sweet corn and chicken.
3. Bring sauce to the boil over gentle heat, stirring continuously.
4. Simmer gently for 5 minutes to ensure chicken is thoroughly re-heated.

*Dolly MacKenzie, East Kilbride*

# Orange Glazed Chicken with Coriander

Pre-heat oven to: 190°C/375°F/Gas5　　Time in oven: 40-45 minutes　　Serves: 4

2 heaped tsp coriander seeds, crushed finely

4 tbs Seville orange marmalade

2 cloves garlic, crushed

1 tsp lemon juice

4 chicken joints or breasts

salt and freshly ground black pepper

1. Mix together crushed coriander seeds, marmalade, garlic and lemon juice.
2. Place chicken in roasting tin, make several cuts in flesh and rub with salt and pepper.
3. Spread marmalade mixture all over chicken, cover and bake in oven.
4. Serve with jacket potato and green salad.

*Mary Ann Murray, Dowanvale, Glasgow*

# Citrus Salmon

Pre-heat oven to: 180°C/350°F/Gas4     Time in oven: 20-25 minutes     Serves: 4

*Sauce*

3 floz/75ml orange juice

grated rind and juice of 1 lime

1 tbs honey

2 tbs oil

**4 pieces fillet of salmon**

**olive oil**

1. Combine sauce ingredients and bring to the boil, stirring with wooden spoon or hand whisk.
2. Heat oil in frying pan and sear salmon on both sides.
3. Put in oven-proof dish and pour sauce over. Bake in oven.
4. Serve with new potatoes and green vegetables or salad.

*Rachel Hunt, Paisley*

# Penne with Trout Fillets

Serves: 6

salt and pepper

flour, to coat trout

6 trout fillets

3 tbs extra virgin olive oil

2 cloves garlic, chopped

$1/2$ tbs rosemary blades, removed from sprig

1 tsp parsley, chopped

$3^1/2$ tbs dry white wine

1 lb/450g penne or any other short pasta

1 tbs lemon juice

thin threads of lemon peel, for decoration

1. Season and flour trout fillets. Cut into pieces about 1"/2.5cm long.
2. Heat oil, add garlic and, when it starts to change colour, add trout, rosemary and parsley.
3. Cook fish lightly on both sides and pour in wine.
4. Cook for a few more minutes, remove from heat and keep warm.
5. Cook pasta in boiling water, drain and stir in lemon juice. Place in individual pasta bowls.
6. Place fish on top with wooden spoon, taking care not to break up fish, pour over sauce.
7. Decorate with strands of lemon peel and serve immediately.

*Marina MacLeod, Livonia, USA*

# Quick Fish Grill

Serves: 4-6

| | |
|---|---|
| 4-6 fish fillets | 11 oz/300g can mandarin oranges |
| salt and pepper | 4 oz/110g grated cheese |

1. Line base of grill pan with foil.
2. Lay fillets on top and season with salt and pepper.
3. Cover with juice and mandarins.
4. Top with grated cheese.
5. Cook under a moderate grill for approximately 10 minutes.

*Dolly Maclean, Leverburgh*

# Spaghetti with Salmon and Dill

Serves: 4

| | |
|---|---|
| 11 oz/325g spaghetti | juice of 1 lemon |
| small packet smoked salmon | 1/2 tbs dill, chopped |
| | 1/4 pt/150ml single cream |

1. Cook pasta in pan of boiling salted water.
2. Cut salmon into strips with scissors and place in bowl with lemon juice and dill.
3. Drain pasta, reserving 2-3 tbs cooking water in bottom of pan.
4. Return pasta to pan with salmon mixture and cream.
5. Season generously with freshly ground black pepper. Serve immediately with salad and crusty bread.

*Fiona MacAskill, St Vincent St/Milton, Glasgow*

# "Chicken" Casserole

Pre-heat oven to: 160°C/325°F/Gas3     Time in oven: 40 minutes     Serves: 4

| | |
|---|---|
| 10 oz/275g can tuna steak | 4 oz/110g mushrooms, sliced |
| 1 can Campbell's chicken soup | 1 cup cooked macaroni, or any pasta |
| 1 can Campbell's mushroom soup | 2 oz/50g almond flakes |

1. Mix all ingredients together.
2. Put in oven-proof casserole dish, cover and bake.

*Anne C Thomson, Dowanvale, Glasgow*

# Baileys Chocolate Cheesecake

Serves: 12-14

*Base*
3 oz/75g margarine
6 oz/175g crushed digestive biscuits

*Filling*
8 oz/225g Philadelphia cheese
1 pt/600ml whipping cream
4 oz/110g dark chocolate
4 floz/110ml Baileys
2 oz/50g icing sugar

1. Melt margarine, add crushed biscuits and press into a greased 10"/22.5cm cake tin with loose base.
2. Whip cheese and cream together until lightly thickened.
3. Melt chocolate in bowl over pan of simmering water.
4. Add Baileys, chocolate and icing sugar to cream and cheese mixture. Mix well.
5. Pour over base and chill.

*Note: This will make a very large cheesecake. Halve the filling ingredients for a smaller one.*

Catriona MacLeod, Lochbroom

# Caramel Bananas

Serves: 4

2 oz/50g brown sugar
2 oz/50g butter
2 tbs cream
1 tsp vanilla essence
4 bananas
1/4 pt/150ml whipping cream

1. Make caramel sauce by heating sugar, butter and cream in pan.
2. Stir for about 4 minutes until thickened. Remove from heat and add vanilla essence.
3. Cut bananas and place in serving dish. Pour sauce over bananas.
4. Whip cream and spread on top.
5. Chill in fridge.

*Note: This makes a delicious pudding in a matter of minutes. For a lower fat version use crème fraîche as an alternative to cream.*

The late Mrs Janet Maclean, Perth

# Banana Surprise

Serves: 2

| | |
|---|---|
| ¹/₄ pt/150ml double cream | I banana |
| ¹/₄ pt/150ml yoghurt | soft brown sugar |

1. Beat cream, add yoghurt and slice in banana.
2. Place in one glass serving dish or individual sundae glasses.
3. Cover with about ¹/₄"/5mm sugar.
4. Leave 4-6 hours or preferably overnight. The sugar melts, caramelizes on top and drizzles down the sides.
5. Serve with wafer biscuits or shortbread fingers.

*Cathie Macleod, Scourie*

# Baked Alaska

Pre-heat oven to: 230°C/450°F/Gas8          Time in oven: 8-10 minutes          Serves: 6

| | |
|---|---|
| I ready-made medium sponge flan case | 4 medium egg whites |
| 18 floz/500ml strawberry ice-cream | 4 oz/110g caster sugar, plus extra to sprinkle |
| | icing sugar and cocoa powder to dust |

1. Place flan case on baking tray lined with grease-proof paper.
2. Spoon ice-cream into flan case and place in freezer.
3. Whisk egg whites in large bowl until stiff and gradually whisk in sugar.
4. Take flan case out of freezer, spoon meringue over ice-cream and smooth over, sealing well at edges where meringue meets flan case.
5. Sprinkle with a little caster sugar and bake until golden.
6. Dust with icing sugar and cocoa powder and serve immediately.

*Margaret Macdonald, Callanish, Lewis*

# Milk Chocolate Cheesecake

Serves: 8-10

| Base | Filling |
|---|---|
| 2 oz/50g butter | 4 oz/110g caster sugar |
| 4 oz/110g digestive biscuits, crushed | I lb/450g Philadelphia cheese |
| | ¹/₂ pt/275ml double cream |
| | 7 oz/200g bar Galaxy/Cadbury's milk chocolate |

1. Melt butter in microwave for 20 seconds. Add crushed digestives and mix.
2. Press into a greased 8"/20cm pie dish and leave to cool.
3. Mix caster sugar and cream cheese together gently.
4. Add double cream and whisk carefully until combined but not too thick.
5. Melt chocolate in microwave for I minute, stir then return to microwave for 30 seconds. Stir until smooth. Leave to cool before mixing into cream mixture.
6. Pour on to biscuit base. Shave some chocolate on top and refrigerate overnight.

*Catherine M Maclennan, Back, Lewis*

# Easy Apple Cake

Pre-heat oven to: 180°C/350°F/Gas4 Time in oven: 1¹/₄ hrs Serves: 8

6 oz/175g S. R. flour
1 level tsp baking powder
2 eggs
6 oz/175g caster sugar
¹/₂ tsp almond essence

4 oz/110g butter, melted and cooled
1 large or 2 medium cooking apples
caster sugar for sprinkling

1. Sift flour and baking powder in a bowl.
2. Beat eggs and sugar until thick and creamy and add essence. Fold in flour and butter.
3. Spread half mixture into a greased and lined loose-based 7"/18cm sandwich tin.
4. Thinly slice apples and arrange in a layer on top of cake mixture. Top with remainder of cake mixture. It does not matter if apples show through.
5. Bake until golden brown and slightly shrunk from sides of tin.
6. Sprinkle with caster sugar while hot.
7. Leave in tin to cool.

*Isobel Hunter, Gairloch*

# Mississippi Mud Pie

Serves: 8

*Base*
3 oz/75g digestive biscuits
3 oz/75g ginger nut biscuits
3 oz/75g butter

*Filling*
8 oz/225g plain chocolate
4 oz/110g marshmallows
¹/₂ pt/300ml double cream
3 tsp Camp coffee
1 tsp rum
¹/₂ tsp cinnamon

1. Melt butter, remove from heat and stir in crushed biscuits.
2. Press crushed biscuits into a greased 9"/23cm loose-based tin.
3. Melt chocolate and marshmallows separately in bowls over pan of boiling water.
4. When cooled, mix together and add double cream.
5. Put coffee into a little hot water and add rum and cinnamon.
6. Gently fold into cream mixture.
7. Spread evenly over base and allow to set in fridge.

*Winifred Harper, Knock E. P. C., N. Ireland*

# Lemon Pots

Serves: 6

10 floz/300ml double cream

9 oz/250g thick natural set yoghurt

I jar good quality lemon curd

4 oz/110g Amaretti or Ratafia biscuits

1. Whisk cream until nearly thick. Fold in yoghurt and lemon curd.
2. Crush biscuits into fairly large pieces in bag with rolling pin.
3. Add to cream mixture.
4. Pour into individual ramekin pots and chill for 2 hours.

*Ruth Macleod, Urray & Strathconnon*

# Raspberry Brulée

Serves: 8

I lb/450g raspberries, fresh or frozen

17 floz/500ml whipping cream

17 floz/500ml carton Greek-style yoghurt

demerara sugar

1. Place raspberries in a shallow serving dish.
2. Whip cream, fold in Greek yogurt and pour mixture over raspberries.
3. Sprinkle demerara sugar thickly and evenly over cream mixture.
4. Chill well in fridge, preferably overnight.
5. Sugar will caramelise in fridge - no need to place under grill.

*Variation: Try a mixture of raspberries and nectarines.*

*Fiona MacArthur, Smithton-Culloden*

# Rice & Pear Meringue

Pre-heat oven to: 170°C/325°F/Gas3          Time in oven: 30 minutes          Serves: 4

17 oz/475g can creamed rice

17 oz/475g can pears

I ½ oz/35g block plain chocolate

2 egg whites

3 oz/75g caster sugar

1. Spoon rice into a greased 8"/20cm diameter, 3"/7.5cm deep oven-proof dish.
2. Drain pears and arrange hollow side up on rice.
3. Break chocolate into small pieces and drop on to pears.
4. Beat egg whites until stiff and carefully fold in sugar.
5. Pile on top of pears and rough up surface with fork.
6. Bake until meringue is crisp on outside.
7. Serve hot.

*Jessie Mary Morrison, North Uist, Grimsay & Berneray*

# Nut Crunch Dessert
Pre-heat oven to: 160°C/325°F/Gas3    Time in oven: 25-30 minutes    Serves: 6-8

3 egg whites
6 oz/175g caster sugar
1/2 tsp baking powder

3 oz/75g walnuts, chopped
2 oz/50g flaked almonds
16 Ritz biscuits, crushed
1/2 tsp vanilla essence
1/2 pt/300ml double cream
small amount crushed nuts to decorate

1. Whisk egg whites until stiff then add sugar and baking powder.
2. Fold in walnuts, almonds, biscuits and vanilla essence.
3. Place in a greased 9"/23cm flan dish.
4. Bake in oven, allow to cool, then decorate with cream and nuts.

*Anne C Thomson, Dowanvale, Glasgow*

# Fruit Crumble
Pre-heat oven to: 180°C/350°F/Gas4    Time in oven: 40 minutes    Serves: 4-6

2 x 14 oz/400g cans of apricot, peaches
  or rhubarb
5 oz/150g plain flour
3 oz/75g margarine

pinch of salt
3 oz/75g demerara sugar
3 oz/75g porridge oats
1 tsp ground cinnamon

1. Rub together flour and margarine in bowl until mixture resembles breadcrumbs.
2. Add salt, sugar and oats.
3. Drain cans of fruit, put fruit in oven-proof dish and spread mixture roughly over fruit.
4. Sprinkle with cinnamon and place in oven. Serve hot.

*Michelle Thomson, East Kilbride*

# Cherry Roll
Serves: 4

1/2 pt/300ml whipping cream
1 packet ginger nut biscuits

1 glass sherry
glacé cherries, for decoration

1. Whip half of the cream until thick.
2. Dip each biscuit in sherry until damp but not soggy.
3. Sandwich biscuits together with whipped cream until all are used, forming a log.
4. Leave overnight in fridge.
5. Whip remainder of cream and cover log.
6. Decorate with cherries.

*Mary Mackenzie, Partick, Glasgow*

# Shortcake

Serves: 6-8

l oz/25g butter
7 oz/200g shortbread, crushed

5 oz/150g white chocolate
¹/2 pt/300ml double cream, lightly whipped
8 oz/225g strawberries or raspberries, chopped

1. Melt butter and stir in crushed shortbread.
2. Melt chocolate, whip cream and fold in melted chocolate.
3. Put half shortbread mix into a greased 8"/20cm flan dish and press mixture down slightly.
4. Spread half chocolate/cream mix on top of shortbread followed by fruit and remainder of chocolate/cream mix.
5. Spread remainder of shortbread mix on top and flatten slightly.
6. Chill for few hours before serving.

*Note: Can be frozen.*

*Alison MacDonald, St Vincent St/Milton, Glasgow*

# "Never-Fail" Pavlova

Pre-heat oven to: 150°C/300°F/Gas2     Time in oven: I hour     Serves: 4-6

2 egg whites
14 oz/400g granulated sugar
I tbs cornflour

I tsp vinegar
I tsp vanilla essence
4 tbs boiling water

1. Whisk egg whites until stiff.
2. Add sugar, cornflour, vinegar, vanilla and boiling water.
3. Whisk until thick and glossy for about 10 minutes.
4. Spread in a circle on non-stick paper and bake.
5. Remove from oven, invert on to cooling tray and carefully remove paper.
6. Transfer on to serving plate and allow to cool. Cover with whipped cream and fruit.

*Margaret Fraser, Lochinver*

# Chocolate Mousse

Serves: 2

7 floz/200ml tub crème fraîche
2 tbs icing sugar

4 oz/110g plain chocolate, melted
fresh orange juice
orange rind

1. Beat crème fraîche and sugar to soft whipped cream thickness.
2. Stir in melted and almost cool chocolate.
3. Put into serving dishes and chill in fridge.
4. When set, squeeze on orange juice and sprinkle a little orange rind over top.

*Effie Lamont, Glenelg, Skye*

 **low fat**

## Chick Pea and Sweet Potato Soup

Serves: 4

2 tbs olive oil
I large onion, finely chopped
I celery stalk, finely chopped
I garlic clove, crushed

I2 oz/350g sweet potato, chopped
I ¼ pt/725ml chicken stock
I tsp basil
I4 oz/400g can chopped tomatoes
I4 oz/400g can chickpeas, drained
2 tbs soy sauce

1. Gently heat olive oil, add onion and celery and cook without colouring for 5 minutes.
2. Add garlic and cook for I minute.
3. Stir in sweet potatoes, stock and basil and bring to the boil.
4. Reduce heat, cover and simmer for 30 to 40 minutes, stirring occasionally.
5. Add tomatoes, chickpeas and soy sauce and simmer for 20 minutes.
6. Add salt and freshly ground black pepper. Purée if desired.

*Note: This soup is best the following day!*

*F. A. MacDonald, Sleat and Strath, Skye*

## Venison Stew

Serves: 4

I ¼ lb/560g diced venison
I tbs oil
I large onion, chopped

2 heaped tbs bramble jelly
7 floz/200ml red wine
7 floz/200ml stock

1. Brown venison in oil.
2. Add onion, place lid on pot and sweat slowly for 20 minutes.
3. Stir in bramble jelly, wine and a little stock. Place lid on pot.
4. Cook slowly for I ½ hours or longer until meat is tender.
5. Check and stir at regular intervals, adding more stock if sauce is getting too dry.

*Debbie MacDonald, Portree, Skye*

# Taunton Pheasant

Serves: 2-4

I pheasant, jointed into 4 pieces
I oz/25g plain flour
salt and freshly ground black pepper
2 tbs olive oil
18 floz/500ml dry cider
I onion, diced
9 floz/250ml Greek yoghurt

*Garnish*
2 dessert apples
parsley
I lemon, sliced thinly
I tbs olive oil

1. If using frozen pheasant, ensure it is completely defrosted.
2. Pull away skin and coat joints in seasoned flour.
3. Heat olive oil in pan and sauté pheasant joints until pale golden.
4. Drain any excess olive oil, stir in cider and bring sauce to the boil.
5. Add onion and simmer gently for 45 minutes.
6. Stir in yoghurt and heat through, but do not allow to boil.
7. Core and slice apples, leaving skin on. Fry gently in olive oil.
8. Arrange pheasant on serving dish and coat with sauce.
9. Garnish with lightly-fried apples, parsley and lemon.

*P. Campbell, Maryburgh & Killearnan*

# Chicken in Creamy Orange Sauce

Serves: 4

4 chicken breast fillets
1/2 pt/300ml orange juice
3 tbs brandy, optional
3 spring onions, chopped

2 tsp cornflour
6 tbs low fat fromage frais
salt and black pepper

1. Fry chicken fillets without fat in non stick pan, turning until evenly browned.
2. Stir in orange juice, brandy, and spring onions.
3. Bring to the boil, cover and simmer for 15 minutes or until chicken is tender and juices run clear when pierced.
4. Blend cornflour with a little water and combine with fromage frais.
5. Pour over chicken and stir over a moderate heat until sauce boils. Simmer for 2 minutes.
6. Season and serve with boiled rice or salad.

*Ena Smith, Free North, Inverness*

# Chilli Mango Chicken Salad

Serves: 4

I red chilli, finely chopped
2 spring onions, finely chopped
2 mangos, peeled and roughly chopped

2 tsp groundnut oil
juice of 2 limes
I crisp lettuce
8 oz/225g cooked chicken

1. Place chopped chilli, spring onions and mango flesh into bowl.
2. Add groundnut oil and lime juice. Put in fridge for I hour or overnight.
3. Roughly tear crisp lettuce leaves.
4. Chop cooked chicken into bite-size pieces.
5. Toss all ingredients together and serve.

*Chris Ann MacLean, Kilmuir, Stenscholl and Snizort, Skye*

# Fish Lasagne

Pre-heat oven to: 190°C/375°F/Gas5     Time in oven: 40-45 minutes     Serves: 4

I tsp polyunsaturated oil
I onion, peeled and finely chopped
4 oz/110g mushrooms
I tsp oregano
14 oz/400g chopped tomatoes
I tbs tomato purée
salt and pepper
I lb/450g cod or haddock fillets, skinned
6-9 sheets lasagne verde

*Topping*
I egg, beaten
4 oz/110g cottage cheese
1/4 pt/150ml low fat natural yoghurt
2 oz/50g half fat cheddar cheese, grated

1. Heat oil in pan, add onions and fry gently until soft.
2. Stir in chopped mushrooms, oregano, chopped tomatoes and their juice.
3. Blend tomato purée with I tbs water, stir into pan and season to taste with salt and pepper.
4. Bring sauce to the boil and simmer uncovered for 5-10 minutes.
5. Remove as many of the tiny pin bones as possible from fish and cut into cubes.
6. Add to tomato sauce mixture and stir gently. Remove pan from heat.
7. Cover base of oven-proof dish with 2-3 sheets of lasagne verde.
8. Top with half of fish mixture. Repeat layers, finishing with lasagne sheets.
9. Mix together beaten egg, cottage cheese and yoghurt. Pour over lasagne and sprinkle with cheese.
10. Cook lasagne in oven until topping is golden brown and bubbling.

*Katie Maclean, Scalpay*

# Slimmers' Goulash

Serves: 4-6

| | |
|---|---|
| 1 ¼ lb/560g lean stewing steak | ¼ pt/150ml stock |
| 1 oz/25g seasoned flour | 14 oz/400g can tomatoes |
| 2 tbs oil, polyunsaturated | 1 tsp tomato purée |
| 1 onion, peeled and thinly sliced | 4 oz/110g peas |
| | 1 tsp paprika |
| | 2 tbs natural yoghurt |
| | salt and pepper |

1. Dice meat, coat with seasoned flour and brown quickly in hot oil.
2. Remove from pan and sauté sliced onion until soft.
3. Return meat to pan and add stock, tomatoes and purée.
4. Cover and simmer for 1 ³/4 hours.
5. Add peas, paprika and seasoning 10 minutes before end of cooking.
6. Remove from heat, stir in yoghurt and serve.

*Katie Maclean, Scalpay*

---

# Low Fat Pork in Spicy Yoghurt Sauce

Pre-heat oven to: 190°C/375°F/Gas5    Time in oven: 30-35 minutes    Serves: 4

| | |
|---|---|
| 4 lean pork steaks | 1 tbs mild curry powder |
| 8 tbs natural yoghurt or low fat crème fraîche | 1 tbs fresh coriander |
| 2 tbs mango chutney | salt and pepper |
| 1 red chilli, finely chopped | |

1. Remove any fat from steaks. Place in an oven-proof dish.
2. Combine remaining ingredients, spoon over steaks, cover and bake.

*Note: Chicken fillets could also be used in place of pork.*

*Laura Fraser, Dingwall*

---

# Fruity Bread Pudding
Pre-heat oven to: 200°C/400°F/Gas6      Time in oven: 25-30 minutes      Serves: 4

3 oz/75g mixed dried fruit  
¹/4 pt/150ml apple juice  
4 oz/110g white bread, diced  
I tsp mixed spice  
I large banana, sliced  

¹/4 pt/150ml skimmed milk  
I tsp demerara sugar  
natural low fat yoghurt  

1. Place dried fruit in small pan with apple juice and bring to the boil.
2. Remove from heat. Stir in bread, spice and banana.
3. Spoon mixture into shallow 2 pt/1.2 litre oven-proof dish and pour over milk.
4. Sprinkle with demerara sugar and bake until firm and golden brown.
5. Serve hot with natural yoghurt.

*Ena Smith, Free North, Inverness*

# Baked Dumpling
Pre-heat oven to: 170°C/325°F/Gas3      Time in oven: 1-1¹/2 hours      Serves: 8-10

8 oz/225g sultanas or raisins  
4 oz/110g soft brown sugar  
I soft sweet apple  
4 oz/110g Flora margarine  
¹/4 pt/150ml water  

3 tbs All Bran  
¹/2 tsp bicarbonate of soda  
8 oz/225g S.R. flour  
pinch of salt  
¹/2 tsp ground cinnamon  
¹/2 tsp mixed spice  

1. Put fruit, sugar, grated apple, margarine and water in pan and bring to the boil.
2. Simmer for about 5 minutes.
3. Add All Bran and leave until lukewarm. Add bicarbonate of soda and stir.
4. Sift flour, salt, cinnamon and mixed spice, add to fruit mixture and mix well.
5. Place in a greased and floured 7"/18cm round cake tin and bake until firm but not over-done.

*Note: Just as good as the real "Clootie" and better for the weight-conscious.*

*Margaret Grant, Falkirk*

# gluten free

## Sweet Potato and Coconut Soup

Serves: 4

2 tbs olive oil

I small onion, chopped

3-4 cloves of garlic, peeled and minced

I tbs fresh ginger, peeled and chopped

I red chilli, deseeded and chopped

14 floz/400ml coconut milk

I lb 5 oz/600g sweet potato, peeled and cubed

I $^3/_4$ pt/I litre vegetable stock

2 tbs of lime or lemon juice

2 tbs fresh coriander, chopped

1. Heat olive oil and stir fry onions for 2-3 minutes.
2. Add garlic, ginger and chilli and continue to stir fry for 1-2 minutes.
3. Pour in coconut milk, stir well and bring to a simmer.
4. Add sweet potato and simmer for 7-8 minutes.
5. Add stock and bring back to a simmer.
6. When sweet potato is tender, blend soup and return to heat.
7. Stir in lime or lemon juice and serve, garnished with coriander.

*Kate Ann Cunningham, Free North, Inverness*

## Carrot and Courgette Loaf

Pre-heat oven to: 180°C/350°F/Gas4          Time in oven: 25-30 minutes          Serves: 4

2 tbs oil

I small onion, finely chopped

2 oz/50g hazelnuts, chopped

4 oz/110g courgettes, coarsely grated

4 oz/110g carrots, coarsely grated

I oz/25g buckwheat flakes

I oz/25g ground almonds

I oz/25g creamed coconut, grated

2 tomatoes, peeled and chopped

I tbs tomato purée

$^1/_2$ tsp dried mixed herbs

$^1/_2$ tsp salt

freshly ground black pepper

1. Heat oil in pan, fry onions and cook gently for 5 minutes.
2. Stir in hazelnuts, carrots and courgettes, cooking for a further 5 minutes.
3. Stir in remaining ingredients.
4. Spoon into a greased and base-lined 1 lb/450g loaf tin.
5. Press down well and bake in oven.
6. Allow to cool for 3 minutes before turning on to serving plate.
7. Serve with home-made tomato sauce and crisp salad.

*Note: Use porridge oats instead of buckwheat flakes if gluten free is not required.*

*Lilian MacDonald, Cumbernauld*

# Risotto

Serves: 4-6

4 tbs oil

I onion, chopped

I red pepper, chopped

I green pepper, chopped

12 oz/350g rice

8 oz/225g can chopped tomatoes, drained

I pt/600ml home-made vegetable stock

5 oz/150g frozen peas

salt and pepper

1. Gently fry onion until soft, add peppers and cook for 3 minutes.
2. Add rice, stirring well until coated in oil.
3. Add tomatoes and stock.
4. Cook over low heat until stock is absorbed, taking approximately 20 minutes.
5. Add peas and seasoning, stir and cook for 2-3 minutes. Serve immediately.

*Rachel Hunt, Paisley*

# Curried Kedgeree

Pre-heat oven to: 180°C/350°F/Gas4     Time in oven: 20 minutes     Serves: 2

I ¹/2 oz/35g butter or margarine

I small onion, finely chopped

2 tomatoes, skinned

I rounded tsp curry powder

¹/2 level tsp salt

pepper

2 oz/50g Basmati rice, cooked

8 oz/225g cooked fish, white or smoked

I raw egg, beaten

I hard boiled egg

*Garnish*

parsley

lemon

egg yolk

1. Melt butter in frying pan, add onion and fry lightly.
1. Add skinned sliced tomato and curry powder and cook for 2 minutes. Add seasoning.
2. Add cooked rice, flaked fish, beaten raw egg and chopped white of hard boiled egg.
3. Place in a greased oven proof dish and bake on middle shelf of oven.
4. Serve in same dish, garnished with sieved hard boiled egg yolk, lemon wedges and parsley.

*Joan Maclean, Lonemore, Skye*

# Raspberry Creams

Serves: 4

8 oz/225g raspberries, can use frozen | I tbs caster sugar

¹/₄ pt/150ml double cream | I tbs demerara sugar

¹/₄ pt/150ml natural yoghurt

1. Reserve 4 raspberries for decoration.
2. Divide rest of raspberries into 4 equal portions in individual stemmed dishes.
3. Whip cream, yoghurt and caster sugar together until stiff.
4. Spoon cream over raspberries.
5. Sprinkle demerara sugar over cream and top with a raspberry.
6. Chill before serving.

*Rachel Hunt, Paisley*

# Chocolate Roulade

Pre-heat oven to: 170°C/325°F/Gas3     Time in oven: 15-20 minutes     Serves: 8-10

7 oz/200g plain dark chocolate, broken up     ³/₄ pt/450ml double cream

3 tbs water     I tbs rum, optional

5 eggs, separated     icing sugar to dust

6 oz/175g caster sugar

1. Line and grease a 15 ¹/₂" x 10 ¹/₂"/38cm x 25cm baking tray.
2. Put chocolate and water in bowl over pan of hot water.
3. Allow chocolate to melt and stir slowly to combine.
4. Whisk egg yolks and sugar until very thick and stir in melted chocolate.
5. Whisk egg whites until stiff and fold into chocolate mixture.
6. Pour into tin and bake until firm.
7. Remove from oven, cover with sheet of grease-proof paper and a damp tea towel. Leave until cold, preferably a couple of hours.
8. Remove towel and paper. Place paper on work surface, dust with icing sugar and invert roulade on to it. Remove lining paper carefully from sponge.
9. Whisk cream and rum and spread over roulade.
10. Roll up from a long edge, like a swiss roll, and place on serving plate.
11. The roulade will crack when rolled. Dust with icing sugar.
12. Cut into slices and serve.

*Note: Add pitted cherries when in season, or tin of cherry pie filling over cream before rolling. Can be frozen.*

*Jane MacLeod, Free North, Inverness*

# Chocolate Orange Cake
Pre-heat oven to: 180°C/350°F/Gas4      Time in oven: I hour      Serves: 12

I large or 2 small oranges

I heaped tsp baking powder

¹/₂ tsp bicarbonate of soda

4 oz/110g cocoa

8 oz/225g ground almonds

10 oz/275g caster sugar

6 eggs

1. Put whole orange in a pan of water and boil until soft, or put in a bowl and microwave on high for approximately 3 minutes.
2. Allow to cool and remove pips.
3. Put into food processor and "pulp".
4. Add remaining ingredients and mix until you have 'cake mixture' consistency.
5. Pour into a greased and base-lined 8"/20cm springform cake tin and bake.
6. Allow to cool in tin and remove carefully.

*Note: If you do not have a processor, chop orange finely and mix with other ingredients.*

*Nikki Galbraith, Campbeltown*

# Scotch Mist
Serves: 6

³/₄ pt/425ml double cream

3 tbs whisky

3 oz/75g meringues, coarsley crushed

I lb/450g strawberries, chopped

6 mint leaves

1. Whip cream with whisky until it just holds its shape.
2. Fold in crushed meringues and chopped strawberries.
3. Spoon mixture into 6 glasses or serving bowls. Cover and chill for about 15 minutes.
4. Decorate with strawberry halves and mint leaves just before serving

*Joan Maclean, Lonemore*

# Empire Biscuits

Pre-heat oven to: 190°C/375°F/Gas5     Time in oven: 15-20 minutes.     Makes: 24

**7 oz/200g gluten-free flour**
**1 oz/25g ground rice**
**1 oz/25g ground almonds**

**5 oz/150g margarine**
**2 oz/50g caster sugar**
**cornflour for rolling**

1. Sieve flour, ground rice and almonds.
2. Add margarine and rub in to form breadcrumbs.
3. Add sugar and knead mixture to form stiff dough.
4. Dust worktop and rolling pin with cornflour. Roll out fairly thinly, cut in 2 1/2"/6mm rounds, place on baking tray and bake.
5. Cool on tray, sandwich together with jam and spread with glacé icing. (See Apple and Walnut cake on page no 105)

*Note: Mixture can be baked in patty tins for fruit tartlets, or used for mince pies with gluten-free mince-meat.*

*Lilian MacDonald, Cumbernauld*

# Coconut Macaroons

Pre-heat oven to: 150°C/300°F/Gas2     Time in oven: 20-25 minutes     Makes: 24

**2 egg whites**
**4 oz/110g icing sugar**

**4 oz/110g desiccated coconut**
**4 oz/110g ground almonds**
**1 tsp almond extract, optional**
**dark plain chocolate for drizzling**

1. Whisk egg whites until stiff. Gently fold in icing sugar.
2. Carefully mix in coconut, ground almonds and almond extract.
3. Using a teaspoon, divide mixture into approximately 24 walnut-size pieces.
4. Place on baking tray lined with grease-proof paper and bake.
5. Macaroons should be lightly browned on outside but soft in the middle.
6. Transfer to cooling tray, melt chocolate and drizzle over.

*Rachel Hunt, Paisley*

# Picnic Slice

Pre-heat oven to: 150°C/300°F/Gas2     Time in oven: 45 mins     Makes: 24 squares

**11 oz/300g dark or milk chocolate**
**3 oz/75g margarine**
**5 oz/150g caster sugar**

**1 egg, beaten**
**5 oz/150g desiccated coconut**
**5 oz/150g sultanas**
**3 oz/75g glacé cherries, chopped**

1. Melt chocolate in bowl over pan of hot water.
2. Pour into a greased and lined 11" x 7"/28cm x 18cm baking tray and allow to set.
3. Cream margarine and sugar and stir in egg, coconut, sultanas and cherries, mixing well.
4. Spoon mixture over chocolate layer and spread with palette knife. Bake until set.
5. Allow to cool. Turn out of tin, carefully peel back greaseproof paper and slice in squares.

*Ishbel Buck, Dowanvale, Glasgow*

# budget

## Sausage Hot Pot

Pre-heat oven to: 200°C/400°F/Gas6          Time in oven: 30 minutes          Serves: 2-3

8 oz/225g small link sausages

1 tbs sunflower cooking oil

1 small carrot, thinly sliced

1 small onion, thinly sliced

1 stick celery, thinly sliced

1 beef stock cube

$1/2$ pt/300ml hot water

1 small can baked beans

2 medium potatoes, sliced

salt and pepper

1. Fry sausages over low heat in oil, until they start to brown.
2. Remove sausages from pan. Place carrot, onion and celery in pan and fry gently.
3. Make up stock in hot water.
4. Place sausages, fried vegetables, stock and beans in casserole dish.
5. Arrange sliced potatoes on top and sprinkle with salt and pepper.
6. Cover with lid or foil and bake in oven.

*Note: Remove foil or lid 10 minutes before end of cooking time to allow potatoes to brown.*

*Margaret McCarrol, Dowanvale, Glasgow*

## Toad in the Hole

Pre-heat oven to: 220°C/425°F/Gas7          Time in oven: 50-55 mins in total          Serves: 4

8 large sausages

1 oz/25g lard/beef dripping

**Batter**

4 oz/110g flour

salt and pepper

2 eggs, beaten

$1/2$ pt/300ml milk

1. Bake sausages with dripping in oven for 15 minutes.
2. Turn sausages occasionally to brown evenly.

*Batter*
1. Sift flour and seasoning into mixing bowl.
2. Pour in eggs and milk and whisk until batter is smooth.
3. Pour batter over sausages while dripping is very hot.
4. Bake for further 40-45 minutes or until batter has risen.
5. Serve immediately with salad.

*Peigi Maclennan, Shawbost, Lewis*

# Macaroni Mince

Pre-heat oven to: 190°C/375°F/Gas5          Time in oven: 30 minutes          Serves: 4-6

1 lb/450g mince

1 large onion, chopped

5 oz/150g can tomato purée

½ pt/300ml stock

6 oz/175g macaroni

**Sauce**

1 oz/25g flour

1 oz/25g margarine

³/4 pt/425ml milk

6 oz/175g grated cheese

1. Brown mince and onion in oil.
2. Add tomato purée and stock, stir and simmer for 15 minutes.
3. Boil macaroni and drain well.
4. Place flour, margarine, milk and seasoning in saucepan and stir or whisk together over low heat until sauce thickens and boils. Simmer gently for 2 minutes.
5. Put layers of meat, sauce, macaroni and cheese into greased oven-proof dish.
6. Pour sauce over top and sprinkle with grated cheese.
7. Bake in oven. Serve with a salad.

*Mary Mackenzie, Partick, Glasgow*

# Chicken Fricassee

Serves: 2

1 cup quick cooking rice

2 cups cold water

2 oz/50g butter

2 oz/50g plain flour

1 pt/600ml milk

salt and pepper

2 chicken breasts, cooked and chopped
   or left-over cooked chicken

1 small can sweetcorn

1. Put rice in to cold water in pan with salt to taste and bring to the boil as quickly as possible. Stir briskly, lower heat and cover pan.
2. Simmer for about 12 minutes until rice is tender but not sticky and all water is absorbed.
3. Melt butter in saucepan on medium heat, add flour and cook, stirring constantly, for 1 minute.
4. Remove from heat and gradually stir in enough milk to make a thick creamy sauce. Season well.
5. Add sweetcorn and chicken and bring back to the boil. Simmer gently for 5 minutes to make sure that chicken is thoroughly heated.
6. Serve with rice and diced carrot or broccoli.

*Michelle Thomson, East Kilbride*

# Potato Scone Pizza

Serves: 2-3

| | |
|---|---|
| I medium boiled potato | *Topping* |
| 4 level tbs S.R. flour | 2 tomatoes |
| salt and pepper | ¹/₂ onion |
| milk to mix | 2 mushrooms |
| I tbs oil or oil spray | ¹/₂ pepper |
| | 2 oz/50g cheese |

1. Mash potato and add flour, seasoning and a little milk to make stiff dough.
2. Roll out to fit 8"/20cm frying pan.
3. Spray pan with oil and heat.
4. Cook pizza base until brown on both sides.
5. Heat grill.
6. Place thinly sliced vegetables on top of pizza base and place under hot grill to cook vegetables.
7. Sprinkle on grated cheese and return to grill until cheese melts.

*Variation: Add a pinch of herbs to base and sprinkle topping with oregano.*

*Katie Campbell, Maryburgh*

# Sausages and Lentils

Serves: 3-4

| | |
|---|---|
| I packet sausages | 7 oz/200g lentils, Puy if possible |
| I tbs olive oil | I garlic clove, crushed |
| 9 oz/250g smoked bacon, chopped | I onion, halved and stuck with 2 cloves |
| | I tsp tomato purée |
| | sprig thyme |
| | I bay leaf |
| | I ³/₄ pt/I litre chicken stock |

1. Grill or fry sausages until cooked and browned. Set to one side.
2. Heat oil in pan and cook bacon until crisp.
3. Add remaining ingredients and simmer gently for 20 minutes.
4. Add sausages and cook for further 10 minutes.
5. Serve with crusty baguette and salad.

*Note: Try Toulouse pork sausages, flavoured with red wine and garlic.*

*May MacAskill, Dunblane*

## Savoury Casserole

Pre-heat oven to: 180°C/350°F/Gas4     Time in oven: 1 hour     Serves: 4

salt and pepper

2 tbs flour

4 x 4 oz/110g pieces liver

5 oz/150g mushrooms, chopped

4 rashers of bacon

1. Season flour, place in polythene bag with liver and shake.
2. Put half of mushrooms in casserole dish.
3. Place liver on top, followed by remaining mushrooms.
4. Cover with rashers of bacon.
5. Place lid on casserole dish and bake in oven.
6. Serve with mashed potatoes and grilled tomatoes.

*C. Macleod, Glendale, Skye*

## Stovies

Serves: 4

1 level tbs dripping or vegetable oil

1 ½ lb/700g potatoes, peeled and sliced

1 large onion, sliced

8 oz/225g sausages or scraps of cold roast beef

½ pt/300ml water or stock

salt and pepper

1. Melt dripping in large pan.
2. Add layer of sliced potatoes, then layer of onion, followed by layer of meat.
3. Add enough water to cover.
4. Repeat layers once again and season.
5. Cover and cook over moderate heat for 30 minutes, shaking pan occasionally, until potatoes are tender and liquid is absorbed.

*Mary Florrie Grant, Poolewe & Aultbea*

## Tomato and Tarragon Sausage Casserole

Pre-heat oven to: 180°C/350°F/Gas4     Time in oven: 45 minutes-1 hour    Serves: 4

1 lb/450g pork sausages

14 oz/400g can chopped tomatoes

4 oz/110g onions, chopped

5 oz/150g carrots, chopped

1 tsp tarragon

3 tbs tomato sauce

½ pt/300ml water

1. Prick sausages with fork and put under grill to brown on both sides.
2. Cut each sausage into 2 or 3 pieces.
3. Put tomatoes, sausages, onions, carrots, tarragon, tomato sauce and water into saucepan, and bring to the boil.
4. Transfer to casserole dish and place in oven.
5. Serve with mashed or baked potatoes and a green vegetable.

*Pam Hart, Strathy & Halladale*

 **international**

## Hot Chicken Curry (Malaysia)

Serves: 4-5

I tbs oil

I large onion, chopped

2 cloves garlic, crushed

I tsp root ginger, grated

I-2 tbs chilli paste, to taste

½ tsp turmeric

2 tsp cumin

I tsp ground coriander

I tbs Chinese 5 spice

I lb/450g potatoes, cubed

2 tbs tomato sauce

I ½ lb/700g diced chicken, breast or thighs

soy sauce, to taste

7 floz/200ml water

1. Heat oil in pan and sauté onion, ginger and garlic for 5 minutes.
2. Add chilli paste and remaining spices and stir till fragrant.
3. Add tomato sauce and cubed potatoes and stir to coat potatoes.
4. Add chicken, soy sauce and water.
5. Cover and simmer until cooked, for about 40 minutes.

*Note: Delicious served with Creamy Coconut Rice*

## Creamy Coconut Rice

I tbs oil

12 oz/350g Basmati rice

14 floz/400ml water

14 floz/400ml can coconut milk

4 shallots, chopped

I clove garlic, crushed

½ tsp salt

1. Heat oil in pan.
2. Add rice and stir to coat in hot oil.
3. Add remaining ingredients and bring to the boil.
4. Simmer with lid on until rice is cooked, for about 10 minutes.

*Szu Shien Ng, Malaysia (SOS Glasgow)*

# Butternut Soup (South Africa)

Serves: 6

2 rashers bacon, chopped

I tbs oil

2 medium onions, chopped

2 cloves garlic, crushed

I lb 2 oz/500g butternut squash, chopped

I potato, chopped

I apple, chopped

I stick of celery, chopped

I tbs lemon juice

1/4 tsp nutmeg

1/2 tsp marjoram

salt and pepper

8 floz/250ml sour cream

1. Fry bacon in pan in a little oil.
2. Add onion and garlic. Sauté for about 5 minutes.
3. Stir in other ingredients, cover and simmer until tender, for about 30 minutes.
4. Liquidize pulp and stir in sour cream.
5. Heat slowly while stirring, but do not boil.

*Morag Christie, King William's Town, SA*

# Dhal Soup (India)

Serves: 4

I oz/25g ghee or butter

I large red onion, peeled and chopped

3 cloves garlic, peeled and sliced

I green chilli, chopped

I tsp cumin powder

4 oz/110g red lentils

I lb 2 oz/400g ripe tomatoes, skinned and chopped

3/4 pt/400ml cold water

salt and pepper

juice of I lemon

I large boiled potato, finely diced

chopped coriander leaves

*Optional garnish*

I floz/30ml olive oil

2 bananas

1. Melt butter in pan and fry onion, garlic, chilli and cumin powder for 5 minutes.
2. Stir in lentils, tomatoes and water.
3. Bring to the boil, reduce heat, cover and simmer until all water is taken up.
4. Mash with fork to break up lentils and season.
5. Add lemon juice and diced potatoes and mix well.
6. Serve in warmed bowls and sprinkle with chopped coriander.

*Optional: Skin and halve bananas lengthways. Heat oil in frying pan, fry bananas on both sides until dark golden and slice thinly. Serve as garnish on soup.*

*Marina Kennedy, Park, Lewis*

# Arroz Con Pollo, Chicken with Rice (Peru)

Serves: 6

2 tbs oil
6 chicken legs
I medium onion, chopped
I clove garlic, crushed
3 oz/75g fresh coriander
4 oz/110g spinach
I tbs water

4 floz/125ml chicken stock
20 floz/600ml water
I 1/4 lbs/560g Basmati rice
6 oz/175g raw diced carrots
6 oz/175g frozen corn
6 oz/175g frozen peas
I tsp salt

1. In large pan, brown chicken legs in oil. Remove from pan.
2. Gently fry onion and garlic in same pan.
3. Blend coriander, spinach and I tbs water.
4. Add to pan with chicken stock and browned chicken legs.
5. Place lid on pan and cook for approximately 15 minutes, until chicken is tender.
6. Remove chicken and keep hot.
7. Add water to liquid left in pan and bring to the boil.
8. Add rice, diced carrots, corn, peas and salt.
9. Stir until liquid returns to the boil. Cover and cook on low heat for approximately 12 minutes, until rice is tender. All liquid should have evaporated.
10. Place rice on serving dish with chicken legs on top.

*Martha Macpherson, Moyobamba, Peru*

# Flygande Jakob, Flying Jacob (Sweden)

Pre-heat oven to: 200°C/400°F/Gas6    Time in oven: 30 minutes    Serves: 4

7 oz/200g smoked bacon
I cooked chicken
1/2 oz/10g butter
2 bananas, sliced
4 1/2 oz/125g peanuts

2-3 tbs tomato ketchup
I tsp chilli powder
1/2 pt/300ml cream
4 oz/110g cheese, grated

1. Fry bacon until almost crispy.
2. Strip chicken from bones and cut into small pieces.
3. Grease oven-proof dish with butter and cover base with bananas.
4. Mix fried bacon and chicken and place on top of bananas.
5. Sprinkle peanuts on top.
6. Mix ketchup and chilli powder into cream and pour over chicken.
7. Top with grated cheese and bake in oven.
8. Serve with rice.

*Henrik Svensson, St Peters, Dundee*

# Peanut Soup, "Inchicapi" in Quechua, "Sopa de Maní" in Spanish (Peru)

Serves: 8

7 oz/200g skinned fresh peanuts

2 tbs chopped red chillies

I medium onion, chopped

3 oz/75g fresh coriander

4 pt/2.4litre water

4 tbs rice

8 chicken breasts

1. Liquidize peanuts, chillies, onion, coriander and 1 pt/600ml water.
2. Put remainder of water in pan and bring to the boil.
3. Add rice, peanut mixture and chicken breasts.
4. Boil gently for 20 minutes, stirring from time to time.
5. Chicken stock may be added if soup gets too thick.

Note: *Traditionally, this is served with the whole piece of chicken in the soup plate, and eaten with a side serving of rice, making it a main course.*
*Alternatively, the chicken may be cut in smaller pieces after cooking has been completed, and returned to the pan, making a substantial soup.*

Martha Macpherson, Moyobamba, Peru

# Jamaican Red Curry

Serves: 6

1 ½ lb/700g tender meat, diced

salt and pepper

I oz/25g butter

I onion, diced

2 tsp curry powder

¼ tsp chilli powder

I tsp garlic powder

I tsp mixed herbs

I tsp oregano

I tsp tomato purée

14 oz/400g tomatoes, chopped

1. Cover bottom of pan with boiling water and add meat and seasoning.
2. Cook on medium heat, stirring slowly until water evaporates.
3. Remove from heat and add butter, onion, spices, tomato purée and chopped tomatoes.
4. Return to heat, mix well and cover saucepan with lid.
5. Simmer for 45 mins-1 hour, stirring occasionally to prevent mixture from sticking.
6. Serve on bed of boiled rice with sliced banana, mandarin oranges, raisins and peanuts.

Vegetarian Option: *Use 1 ½ lbs/700g diced vegetables and reduce cooking time to 30 minutes.*

Yvette Ellis, Ayr

# La Tapenade (France)

Serves: 8

4 garlic cloves, crushed

7 oz/200g green olives

4 anchovies from a jar

4 oz/110g capers

8 floz/250ml olive oil

juice 1/2 lemon

pepper

8 thin slices bread

1/2 garlic clove

1. Blend together all ingredients, apart from bread and garlic clove, to make thick paste.
2. Toast bread and rub with garlic clove.
3. Put paste on top of toast and cut into triangles.
4. Serve as a starter.

*Catherine Welsh, Bon Accord, Aberdeen*

# 'Asado', Peruvian Beef

Serves: 6-8

2 lb/900g topside or silverside

2 tbs oil

2 onions

3 tomatoes

1 red pepper, seeded

4 medium carrots

2 bay leaves

salt and pepper

1/2 glass red wine, optional

1. Heat oil in heavy-based pan and brown meat.
2. Chop vegetables in big chunks, tomatoes and onions in eighths and peppers and carrots in quarters. Add to pan.
3. Add bay leaves, wine and seasoning.
4. Cover, boil for 2 minutes and simmer for approximately 2 hours, turning meat from time to time.
5. Once everything is well cooked, remove bay leaves and meat and liquidize vegetables and gravy. Check seasoning. Gravy should be thick.
6. Serve with potatoes, rice or pasta.

*Note: Do not add any water or stock. Ideal for slow cookers.*

*Anita Lamont, Dornoch*

# Le Far Breton, Cake from Brittany (France)

Pre-heat oven to: 240°C/475°F/Gas9     Time in oven: 35 mins in total     Serves: 10

9 oz/250g demerara sugar

4 medium eggs

9 oz/250g plain flour

¹/₂ tbs vegetable oil

35 floz/l litre full fat milk

¹/₂ tsp salt

¹/₂ oz/10g butter

9 oz/250g stoned prunes

1. Lightly whisk together sugar and eggs. Whisk in flour.
2. Add oil, milk and salt and mix well.
3. Grease 1 large oven-proof dish with butter and pour in mixture.
4. Cook for 5 minutes then reduce oven to 170°C/325°F/Gas3.
5. Take out of oven and add prunes.
6. Cook for further 30 minutes at lower temperature until golden brown on top.
7. Allow to cool then place in fridge, where mixture will set.
8. Serve cold with cream as a dessert, or as a cake with freshly brewed coffee.

*Note: Can be kept in the fridge for 3 days.*

Catherine Welsh, Bon Accord, Aberdeen

# Papa a la Huancaina (Peru)

Serves: 6 as a starter

2 lbs/900g potatoes

2 fresh yellow chillies

5 oz/150g cottage cheese

2 floz/50ml milk

1 clove garlic, crushed

1 small onion

4 cream crackers, finely crushed

salt and pepper

**Garnish**

few lettuce leaves

¹/₂ boiled egg

1 olive

1. Boil unpeeled potatoes. Set to one side to cool.
2. Halve chillies, remove seeds and stalks and boil for 3 minutes. Peel.
3. Liquidize peeled chillies, cheese, milk, garlic, onion and cream cracker crumbs. Add seasoning.
4. Peel and thickly slice cold potatoes, place on serving dish and pour over liquidized mixture.
5. Garnish with lettuce, boiled egg and an olive.

*Note: The cream also makes an excellent dip.*

Julia Smith, Lima, Peru

# Papas chorreadas, Potatoes with Cheesy Sauce (Colombia)
Serves: 8

3 lbs/1.35kg red-skinned potatoes

2-3 dsp oil

8 spring onions, 7 chopped

2 tomatoes, chopped

$^1/_2$ chicken stock cube, crumbled

I dsp coriander, finely chopped

salt

pinch of cumin

$^1/_4$ tsp paprika

4 floz/125ml milk

4 floz/125ml cream

$^1/_2$ lb/450g Mozzarella cheese, grated

1. Wash potatoes and remove blemishes.
2. Place in pan, cover with water and add salt and I spring onion.
3. Boil until tender and before skins come off. Drain.
4. Put oil in big pan and fry chopped spring onions, but do not brown.
5. Stir in tomatoes, stock cube, coriander, salt, cumin and paprika.
6. Add milk and cream.
7. Transfer potatoes to serving dish.
8. Add cheese to sauce and stir until cheese melts. Quickly pour over potatoes and serve.

*Patty Reaño, Medellin, Colombia*

# Roast Plantains (Colombia)
Serves: 4-5

3 plantains (tropical fruit resembling bananas)

oil for deep frying

1. Peel plantains and cut into 2$^1/_2$"/5cm chunks.
2. Deep fry a few at a time, depending on size of pan.
3. When they float to surface, lift on to kitchen paper to drain.
4. Using base of tumbler, flatten fried pieces. They will now look something like a sunflower in shape!
5. Deep fry again until they float and are crisp.
6. Drain and serve, sprinkled with salt.

*Carlos Lozano, Cali, Colombia via St Vincent St/Milton, Glasgow*

 # snacks

## Bacon and Egg Rice

Serves: 4

| | |
|---|---|
| 1 onion, chopped | 12 oz/350g can sweetcorn, drained |
| 7 oz/200g bacon, chopped | 8 oz/225g long grain rice |
| oil | 2 eggs, beaten |

1. Fry chopped onion and bacon in a little oil in wok or large frying pan until cooked.
2. Boil rice until grains are cooked but not too soft then drain.
3. Add cooked rice to onion and bacon and stir.
4. Add sweetcorn and stir in beaten eggs. Stir until eggs are cooked.
5. Serve.

*Joyce Macleod, Back, Lewis*

## Quick Chicken Tartlets

Pre-heat oven to: 190°C/375°F/Gas5     Time in oven: 30 minutes     Makes: 24

| *Shortcrust pastry* | *Filling* |
|---|---|
| 8 oz/225g plain flour | 4 oz/110g Cheddar cheese, finely grated |
| pinch of salt | 6 oz/175g cooked chicken, chopped |
| 4 oz/110g block margarine | 2 sticks celery, chopped |
| 3 tbs cold water | 5 tbs mayonnaise |
| | salt and pepper |

1. Sieve together flour and salt. Rub in margarine until mixture resembles fine breadcrumbs.
2. Add water and mix to form stiff dough. Knead pastry on floured surface and roll out thinly.
3. Cut 24 circles and use to line patty tins.
4. Mix together cheese, chicken, celery, mayonnaise, salt and pepper.
5. Divide mixture between patty tins.
6. Bake in oven. Serve hot or cold.

*Katie Campbell, Maryburgh & Killearnan*

# Cheese Puffs
Pre-heat oven to: 230°C/450°F/Gas8       Time in oven: 10 minutes       Makes: 12

2 oz/50g Cheddar cheese, grated
1 oz/25g Parmesan cheese, grated
3 oz/75g plain flour
salt and pepper

7 floz/200ml cold water
2 oz/50g butter
2 eggs, well whisked
1 tsp baking powder

1. Grease bun tray or insert paper cases.
2. Season flour with salt and pepper and gradually stir in cold water.
3. Melt butter in a pan, add flour mixture and stir. Simmer for 5 minutes.
4. Remove from heat and stir in Cheddar cheese. Beat in eggs and stir in baking powder.
5. Drop dessertspoonfuls of mixture on to bun tray and sprinkle on Parmesan cheese.
6. Bake until browned.

*Isobel Stewart, Sleat & Strath, Skye*

# Chicken Salad
Serves: 6

1 lb/450g chicken breasts, cooked
6 oz/175g celery, chopped
5 oz/150g seedless grapes, halved
4 oz/110g dried apricots, chopped
2 tbs parsley, chopped

8 floz/250ml mayonnaise
8 floz/250ml plain yoghurt
1 tbs Dijon mustard
salt and pepper

1. Chop chicken into chunks.
2. Combine all ingredients and serve.

*Note: Delicious on croissants.*

*Dana Evans, Nairn*

# Lewis Quiche
Pre-heat oven to: 180°C/350°F/Gas4       Time in oven: 40 minutes       Serves: 8

12 oz/350g courgettes, grated
3 rashers bacon, chopped
6 oz/175g carrots, grated
1 onion, chopped finely
4 oz/110g cheese, grated

½ tsp ground nutmeg
3 tbs cooking oil
salt and pepper
3 oz/75g S.R. flour
4 eggs, well beaten

1. Mix above ingredients in bowl.
2. Place in a greased 9"/23cm diameter flan dish.
3. Bake in centre of oven.

*Note: Eat hot or cold. Can be frozen.*

*Marie C Gillies, Stornoway, Lewis*

# Moira's Pizza Buns

Pre-heat oven to: 190°C/375°F/Gas3    Time in oven: 20 minutes    Makes: 20

8 oz/225g S.R. flour

4 oz/110g margarine

3 oz/75g Cheddar cheese

1 tomato, chopped

1 onion, chopped

6 rashers streaky bacon, chopped

1 egg

1. Rub margarine into flour until mixture resembles fine breadcrumbs.
2. Add cheese, tomato, onion and bacon.
3. Bind together with egg.
4. Place "dollops" as for rock buns on baking parchment on baking tray.
5. Bake until golden brown.  Serve while still warm.

*Ibby MacIver, Maryburgh & Killearnan*

# Smoked Salmon Baguette

1 baguette

caramelised red peppers

Salar flaky smoked salmon

sliced Brie cheese

sliced avocado

rocket leaves, or shredded lettuce

salad dressing

1. Split baguette lengthways and hinge top back.
2. Construct filling as follows: lettuce, avocado, cheese, salmon and red pepper.
3. Sprinkle with salad dressing.

*Note: Salar flaky smoked salmon is one of the nicest but any smoked salmon will do.  This is a great lunch and very filling.  Serve with a chilled Chardonnay.*

*Eric Paterson, Golspie*

# Self-Crusting Quiche

Pre-heat oven to: 180°C/350°F/Gas4    Time in oven: 30 minutes    Serves: 4-6

3 eggs, beaten

1 tsp melted butter

1 onion, chopped

1/2 tsp mixed herbs

2-3 rashers bacon, chopped

4 oz/110g grated cheese

1/2 pt/300ml milk

2 oz/50g S.R. flour

2 medium potatoes, cooked and cubed

1. Mix all ingredients in a bowl.
2. Spread into a greased 9"/23cm round casserole dish.
3. Place in oven and cook until browned.

*Margaret Campbell, Duthil-Dores*

 **baking**

## Anzac Biscuits

Pre-heat oven to: 150°C/300°F/Gas2    Time in oven: 20 minutes    Makes: 34-36

3 ½ oz/85g rolled oats
2 ½ oz/60g desiccated coconut
4 oz/110gplain flour
7 oz/200gsugar

2 tbs golden syrup
4 oz/110g butter
½ tsp bicarbonate of soda
1 tbs water

1. Mix together oats, coconut, flour and sugar.
2. Melt syrup and butter together.
3. Mix bicarbonate of soda with boiling water and add to melted butter and syrup.
4. Add to dry ingredients.
5. Place tbs of mixture on greased tray, allowing room for spreading.
6. Loosen while warm and cool on trays.

*Nicole Madden, London*

## Coconut Rings

Pre-heat oven to: 190°C/375°F/Gas5    Time in oven: 20 minutes    Makes: 15-16

2 oz/50g butter
2 oz/50g margarine
3 oz/75g caster sugar
½ oz coconut
1 egg

5 oz/150g S.R. flour
½ tsp lemon juice
coconut to coat
glacé cherries, halved

1. Cream fats and caster sugar. Add coconut and beaten egg.
2. Fold in flour, then lemon juice.
3. Make 15-16 small balls, roll them in coconut and place on a greased baking tray.
4. Press down in centre to make a hollow and place a half cherry on each.
5. Bake until they are light brown.

*Martha Munro, Smithton-Culloden*

# Auntie Betty's Shortbread

Pre-heat oven to: 150°C/300°F/Gas2   Time in oven: 45 mins-1 hour   Makes: 36 triangles

**4 oz/110g soft margarine, Stork or Flora**      **5 oz/150g caster sugar**
**9 oz/250g Kerrygold butter**                    **1 lb/450g Bero plain flour**

1. Place margarine and butter in mixing bowl, add sugar and mix together.
2. Add flour and beat well until light and fluffy.
3. Divide mixture into three 8"/20cm round tins.
4. Spread into tins with a palette knife and prick with a fork.
5. Bake until just beginning to change colour.
6. Switch off oven, cut into triangles and sprinkle with caster sugar.
7. Return shortbread to oven and allow to cool.

*Margaret Smith, Bon Accord, Aberdeen*

# Skogheim Cookies

Pre-heat oven to: 180°C/350°F/Gas4        Time in oven: 12 minutes      Makes: 16-20

**4 oz/110g plain flour**            **5 oz/150g margarine**
**6 oz/175g white sugar**           **1 egg**
**1 tsp baking powder**             **vanilla essence**
**1/2 tsp bicarbonate of soda**     **4 oz/110g porridge oats**
**4 oz/110g brown sugar**           **2 oz/50g coconut**

1. Sift flour, white sugar, baking powder and bicarbonate of soda.
2. Add brown sugar.
3. Rub margarine into flour until mixture resembles fine breadcrumbs.
4. Mix together egg, vanilla essence, oats and coconut.
5. Add to rubbed-in mixture and mix together.
6. Roll into balls and press down on to tray with fork dipped in flour. Bake.
7. Allow to cool on tray.

*Sandra Glover, Livingston*

# Apple and Walnut Cake

Pre-heat oven to: 180°C/350°F/Gas4     Time in oven: 40-45 mins     Makes: 12-14 slices

| | |
|---|---|
| 3 oz/75g margarine | 2 oz/50g walnuts |
| 5 oz/150g caster sugar | 2 oz/50g raisins |
| 2 eggs, beaten | 1 apple, diced |
| 7 oz/200g plain flour | 2 tbs milk |
| 2 ¹/₂ level tsp baking powder | *Glacé Icing* |
| ¹/₂ tsp salt | 4 oz/110g icing sugar |
| ¹/₂ tsp cinnamon | 1-1 ¹/₂ tbs warm water |
| pinch of nutmeg | |

1. Cream margarine and sugar and add beaten eggs with a little flour.
2. Add remaining dry ingredients.
3. Fold in walnuts, raisins, apple and milk.
4. Spoon into a greased and lined 2 lb/900g loaf tin.
5. Bake until nicely browned and firm to the touch.
6. Sift icing sugar into bowl and add water. Stir with wooden spoon until smooth.
7. When cold, decorate with glacé icing and walnuts.

*Julie Ross, Wick*

# Boiled Fruit Cake

Pre-heat oven to: 160°C/325°F/Gas3     Time in oven: 1 ¹/₄-1 ¹/₂ hrs     Makes: 20 slices

| | |
|---|---|
| 1 lb 2 oz/500g dried mixed fruit | 2 large eggs, lightly beaten |
| 5 floz/150ml sherry or brandy | 5 oz/150g S.R. flour |
| ¹/₂ pint/300ml water | 5 oz/150g plain flour |
| 4 oz/110g butter | ¹/₂ tsp mixed spice |
| 2 tbs golden syrup | ¹/₄ tsp nutmeg |
| 5 oz/150g dark brown sugar | 1 tsp vanilla essence |
| 1 tsp bicarbonate of soda | blanched almonds to decorate |
| 1 tbs boiling water | |

1. Soak fruit overnight in sherry or brandy.
2. Place soaked fruit, water, butter, golden syrup and sugar in a saucepan.
3. Slowly bring to the boil. Allow to cool for 15 minutes, stirring occasionally.
4. Add bicarbonate of soda mixed with water.
5. Add eggs, mixing thoroughly.
6. Fold in sieved flours, spices and vanilla essence.
7. Place in a lined 8"/20cm diameter cake tin
8. Decorate with almonds and bake in oven.
9. Allow to cool in tin for a few minutes before transferring to cooling tray.

*Mary B Macleod, Knock, Lewis*

# Apricot Cake

Pre-heat oven to: 170°C/325°F/Gas3        Time in oven: 1-1 1/2 hours        Serves: 4-6

4 oz/110g soft margarine

4 oz/110g caster sugar

2 eggs, beaten

1/4 tsp vanilla essence

8 oz/225g S. R. flour, sieved

14 oz/400g can apricot halves, drained and chopped

8 oz/225g sultanas

1. Cream margarine and sugar. Beat in eggs and vanilla.
2. Fold in flour, apricots and sultanas.
3. Spoon into a greased and lined 7"/18cm round cake tin. Level top and bake.
4. When ready, cake should spring back when gently pressed in the middle.
5. Turn out on to cooling tray.

*Jessie Mary Morrison, North Uist, Grimsay and Berneray*

# Cake Number 14

Makes: 14 slices!

14 marshmallows, chopped

2 oz/50g margarine

14 cherries, chopped

14 digestive biscuits, crushed

14 walnuts, chopped

1 small can condensed milk

4 oz/110g desiccated coconut

1. Use kitchen scissors or hot knife to cut marshmallows.
2. Melt margarine, add cherries, biscuits, marshmallows and walnuts and mix well.
3. Add milk to bind together.
4. Form into a log and roll in coconut.
5. Put in fridge to set and cut into slices.

*Sheena G. K. Macdonald, South Uist & Benbecula*

# Quick Christmas Cake

Pre-heat oven to: 150°C/300°F/Gas2        Time in oven: 2 1/2 hours        Makes: 30 slices

8 oz/225g plain wholemeal flour

3 tsp baking powder

5 oz/150g soft margarine

5 oz/150g dark brown sugar

6 oz/175g mixed fruit

zest of 1 lemon and 1 orange

2 oz/50g walnuts

3 eggs

1 lb/450g mincemeat

1. Place all ingredients in mixing bowl and cream well together.
2. Spoon into a lined 8"/20cm diameter cake tin and bake in oven.
3. Remove carefully from tin and cool on wire rack.

*Note: Can be eaten immediately, does not require time to mature.*

*Mary Smith, Dowanvale, Glasgow*

# Christmas Wine Cake

Pre-heat oven to: 170°C/325°F/Gas3    Time in oven: 2¹/₂ hrs in total    Makes: 40 slices

6 oz/175g sultanas
6 oz/175g raisins
4 oz/110g currants
Soak the above six ingredients together for 1 week.

3 oz/75g cherries
3 oz/75g mixed peel
¹/₂ pt/300ml sherry

6 oz/175g butter
6 oz/175g soft brown sugar
4 eggs, beaten

4 oz/110g S.R. flour
4 oz/110g plain flour
1 tsp mixed spice
1 oz/25g ground almonds
pinch of salt

1. Cream butter and sugar.
2. Add beaten eggs and remaining dry ingredients.
3. Mix well and add fruit mixture.
4. Bake in a lined 8"/20cm square tin for 1 hour then 1¹/₂ hours at 150°C/300°F/Gas2.
5. Remove carefully from tin and cool on wire rack.

*P. Nicholson, North Uist, Grimsay and Berneray*

# Cherry and Coconut Cake

Pre-heat oven to: 180°C/350°F/Gas4    Time in oven: 1-1¹/₄ hrs    Makes: 20 slices

12 oz/350g S.R. flour
a pinch of salt
6 oz/150g margarine

8 oz/225g glacé cherries, quartered
2 oz/50g desiccated coconut
6 oz/175g caster sugar
¹/₄ pt/150ml milk
2 eggs, lightly beaten

1. Sieve flour and salt and rub in margarine.
2. Toss cherries in coconut and add to mixture with sugar.
3. Add milk to eggs and stir into mixture.
4. Spoon into a lined 8"/20cm diameter cake tin. If desired, sprinkle extra coconut on top. Bake.

*Note: If desired, use blueberries instead of cherries.*

*Moira Westland, Mull*

# Chocolate Orange Cake

Pre-heat oven to: 180°C/350°F/Gas4     Time in oven: 50 minutes     Serves: 12

3 eggs
5 oz/150g S.R. flour, sifted
1 oz/25g cocoa powder, sifted
6 oz/175g caster sugar
6 oz/175g butter, softened

*Butter Cream*
3 oz/75g butter, softened
6 oz/175g icing sugar, sifted
2 tbs milk
1 oz/25g chocolate orange, melted

*Cake*
1. Beat together eggs, flour, cocoa, caster sugar and butter for 2 minutes or until blended.
2. Spoon mixture into a greased and lined 2 lb/900g loaf tin. Level surface, making a slight well in centre.
3. Bake until spongy to the touch. Turn out on to cooling tray.

*Butter Cream*
1. Beat butter, icing sugar and milk until smooth.
2. Divide into 2 bowls.
3. Melt chocolate and fold into 1 bowl of butter cream.
4. Spoon both butter creams over top of cooled cake and swirl gently with a palette knife.

*Note: Use plain chocolate if you do not have chocolate orange.*

*Dolly J. MacLeod, Barvas, Lewis*

# Chocolate Cake

Pre-heat oven to: 180°C/350°F/Gas4     Time in oven: 40 minutes     Serves: 8-10

2 oz/50g cocoa
6 tbs boiling water
6 oz/175g S.R. flour
1 tsp baking powder
6 oz/175g sugar
6 oz/175g soft margarine
2 eggs, beaten

*Icing*
4 oz/110g icing sugar
2 oz/50g margarine
2 tsp milk
2 tsp cocoa powder

*Sponge*
1. Blend cocoa powder with boiling water.
2. Place mixture in a bowl with flour, baking powder, sugar, margarine and eggs.
3. Whisk until light and fluffy.
4. Spread evenly in a greased and lined 7"/18cm diameter cake tin and bake.

*Icing*
1. Cream together and spread over cake when cold.

*Morag MacKinnon, Sleat and Strath, Skye*

# Coffee and Walnut Sponge

Pre-heat oven to: 180°C/350°F/Gas4      Time in oven: 30 minutes      Serves: 10-12

6 oz/175g butter or margarine

6 oz/175g caster sugar

4 eggs

6 oz/175g S.R. flour

1/2 tsp baking powder

2 oz/50g crushed walnuts

I tsp instant coffee, diluted in a little water

*Filling*

4 oz/110g butter or margarine

3 oz/75g icing sugar

I tsp instant coffee, dissolved in a little water

*Sponge*
1. Cream butter and sugar.
2. Add eggs one at a time, beating well in between.
3. Sift in flour and baking powder.
4. Add walnuts and coffee, folding in carefully.
5. Divide between 2 greased and base-lined 8"/20cm diameter sponge tins and bake.
6. Remove from tins and place on cooling tray.

*Filling*
1. Cream together butter, icing sugar and coffee
2. Use to sandwich cooled sponges together.

*Uisdean Ross, Hilton, Fearn*

# Lemon Curd Cake

Pre-heat oven to: 140°C/275°F/Gas1      Time in oven: I hour      Serves: 12

5 oz/125g butter

5 oz/125g caster sugar

3 eggs

8 oz/225g S.R. flour, sifted

1/2 jar lemon curd

*Water Icing*

6 tbs icing sugar, sifted

I tbs water

*Cake*
1. Cream butter and sugar together until light and fluffy.
2. Add eggs one at a time with flour, beating well.
3. Fold in lemon curd.
4. Pour mixture into a greased and lined 8"/20cm round cake tin and bake until brown and firm to touch.
5. When cool, cover top with water icing.

*Water Icing*
1. Mix together and stir until smooth.

*Margaret McNeill, Tarbert, Loch Fyne*

# Crunchy Malteser Cake

Makes: 12 slices

2 oz/50g butter

2 tbs syrup

2 tbs cocoa

6 oz/175g rich tea biscuits

6 oz/175g Maltesers

1. Melt butter and syrup and add cocoa.
2. Roughly crush biscuits and stir into butter mixture.
3. Crush half Maltesers and add along with remaining Maltesers.
4. Put mixture into piece of cling film or foil.
5. Mould into a sausage shape and place in fridge for about 2 hours.
6. Cut into slices and serve.

*Note: As an alternative, Maltesers can be replaced with marshmallows.*

*Joan Beaton, Oban*

# My Mum's Macaroon Round

Pre-heat oven to: 180°C/350°F/Gas4     Time in oven: 35 minutes     Serves: 8-10

*Shortcrust Pastry*

4 oz/110g S.R. flour

pinch of salt

2 oz/50g margarine

1 ½ tbs cold water

*Filling*

2 level tbs raspberry jam

1 teacup semolina

1 level tsp baking powder

1 teacup sugar

1 egg, beaten

1 tsp almond essence

1. See recipe for shortcrust pastry on page no 137.
2. Knead dough gently on floured surface and roll out slightly larger than baking tin.
3. Line a greased 8"/20cm round sponge tin with shortcrust pastry and spread with jam.
4. Mix other filling ingredients together and put into pastry base.
5. Bake on bottom shelf of oven.

*Note: Can also be made into individual cakes rather than one large round.*

*Daphne Douglas, Leith*

# New Zealand Sultana Cake

Pre-heat oven to: 160°C/325°F/Gas3 | Time in oven: 1 hour | Serves: 20

1 lb/450g sultanas
8 oz/225g butter
8 oz/225g sugar
3 eggs

12 oz/350g plain flour
1 tsp baking powder
1 tsp lemon essence

1. Cover sultanas with water and boil for 15 minutes. Drain.
2. Melt butter and add sugar mixed with eggs.
3. Sift in flour and baking powder.
4. Mix in essence.
5. Bake in a greased and lined 8"/20cm round cake tin.
6. When cooked, remove from tin and place on cooling rack.

*Marion MacKellar, Strachur*

# Parsnip Cake

Pre-heat oven to: 150°C/300°F/Gas2 | Time in oven: 1 ½-2 hrs | Makes: 10 slices

3 eggs
6 floz/175ml sunflower oil
2 tsp vanilla essence
2 floz/50ml soured cream
12 oz/350g muscovado sugar
9 oz/250g flour
1 tsp nutmeg
2 level tsp cinnamon
1 tsp bicarbonate of soda
½ tsp salt
11 oz/300g parsnips, peeled & grated
3 oz/75g desiccated coconut

*Topping*
6 oz/175g cream cheese
4 oz/110g icing sugar
grated rind and juice of 1 lime/lemon

1. In one bowl place eggs, oil, vanilla essence and soured cream.
2. Add sugar and stir well.
3. Into another bowl sift flour, nutmeg, cinnamon, soda and salt.
4. Beat wet ingredients and sugars together and fold in dry ingredients, followed by parsnips and coconut. Mix well.
5. Pour into a lined 8"/20cm round cake tin and bake until centre of cake springs back when pressed gently in the middle. Cool on wire rack.
6. Cream together cheese and icing sugar, add lemon juice and spread thickly on top.

*Note: Can be made with carrots instead of parsnips.*

*Daphne Colpman, London*

# The Castles Chocolate Mocha Cake
Pre-heat oven to: 170°C/325°F/Gas3     Time in oven: 40 minutes     Serves: 10-12

6 ½ oz/190g S. R. flour
5 oz/150g caster sugar
2 eggs
¼ pt/150ml oil
¼ pt/150ml milk
1 tsp bicarbonate of soda
2 tbs golden syrup
2 tbs cocoa

*Icing*
3 oz/75g soft margarine
8 oz/225g icing sugar, sieved
1 tbs milk
1 tbs coffee essence
chocolate flake or grated chocolate

1. Blend all ingredients together until smooth.
2. Pour into 2 greased and base-lined 8"/20cm diameter sandwich tins and bake.
3. When ready, cake springs back when pressed lightly in the middle.
4. Cool on wire tray and remove paper.
5. Place all icing ingredients in a bowl and beat until smooth.
6. Spread ⅓ of this mixture on one cake and put the other cake on top.
7. Cover top with remaining icing and mark attractively with a palette knife.
8. Decorate with chocolate flake or grated chocolate.

*Mrs Joan Campbell, Bracadale, Skye*

# Tropical Fruit Cake
Pre-heat oven to: 175°C/350°F/Gas 4     Time in oven: 35-40 mins     Makes: 20-30 slices

5 oz/150g mixed dried tropical fruit
4 oz/110g pineapple juice
8 oz/225g wholemeal flour
2 tsp baking powder
pinch of salt
1 tsp ground ginger

7 oz/200g margarine or butter
4 oz/110g light brown sugar
2 large eggs, beaten

1. Soak dried fruit in pineapple juice for 10 minutes.
2. Sieve together flour, baking powder, salt and ginger in bowl.
3. Rub in margarine until mixture resembles fine breadcrumbs.
4. Stir in sugar and add fruit, juice and beaten eggs.
5. Mix to a soft dropping consistency, adding a little extra pineapple juice or milk as required.
6. Spoon mixture into a greased and lined 7"/18cm diameter cake tin. Bake.
7. Cool briefly in tin and turn out on to wire rack to cool completely.

*Jill Baxter, Cumbernauld*

# Banana and Chocolate Chip Muffins

Pre-heat oven to: 200°C/400°F/Gas6    Time in oven: 20-25 minutes    Makes: 12

10 oz/275g plain flour
1 tsp baking powder
1 tsp bicarbonate of soda
2 oz/50g plain chocolate chips

3 large well-ripened bananas
3 oz/75g granulated sugar
1 egg, beaten
2 floz/50ml milk or water
3 floz/90ml corn oil

1. Grease muffin tray or insert paper cases.
2. In a large bowl, sieve together flour, baking powder and bicarbonate of soda then add chocolate chips.
3. In another bowl, mash bananas thoroughly with a potato masher.
4. Add sugar, beaten egg, water and oil. Stir well.
5. Pour wet ingredients into dry. Stir until just combined. Batter will be lumpy, but no dry flour should be visible.
6. Spoon into muffin tray. Bake until tops are lightly browned and spring back when pressed.

*Ailie Holmes, Bon Accord, Aberdeen*

# Bran Muffins

Pre-heat oven to: 200°C/400°F/Gas6    Time in oven: 10-12 minutes    Makes: 24

6 oz/175g plain wholemeal flour
1 tsp salt
6 tbs wheatgerm
2 tsp baking powder
3 oz/75g natural bran
2 oz/50g caster sugar
1 oz 25g sunflower seeds

1 tbs treacle
2 eggs
6 tbs vegetable oil
2 oz/50g raisins
2 oz/50g sesame seeds
3/4 pt/450ml milk

1. Grease a muffin tray or insert paper cases.
2. Put all dry ingredients in large bowl.
3. Add treacle, eggs, oil, raisins, sunflower seeds and milk and lightly mix together. Mixture should be quite soft.
4. Spoon mixture into muffin tray and sprinkle tops with sesame seeds.
5. Bake until tops are lightly browned and spring back when pressed.
6. Remove from tray while still hot.
7. Serve with butter and honey or jam.

*Helen MacRae, Poolewe & Aultbea*

# Carrot and Pineapple Muffins

Pre-heat oven to: 180°C/350°F/Gas4     Time in oven: 25-30 minutes     Makes: 18

8 oz/225g plain flour

8 oz/225g sugar

I tsp baking powder

I tsp bicarbonate of soda

1/2 tsp salt

I tsp cinnamon

5 floz/150ml cooking oil

2 eggs

8 oz/225g grated raw carrot

4 floz/125ml crushed pineapple with juice

I tsp vanilla essence

1. Grease or line muffin tray with paper cases.
2. Sift flour, sugar, baking powder, bicarbonate of soda, salt and cinnamon.
3. Make well in centre of dry ingredients.
4. Combine oil, eggs, carrot, pineapple and vanilla essence. Stir into dry ingredients.
5. Spoon batter to half fill cups.
6. Bake until golden brown.

*Annie Matheson, Desable, P.E.I.*

# Mincemeat Muffins

Pre-heat oven to: 200°C/400°F/Gas6     Time in oven: 20-25minutes     Makes: 12

10 oz/275g plain flour

2 tsp baking powder

1/2 tsp bicarbonate of soda

1/2 tsp salt

3 oz/75g fine granulated sugar

I egg

12 oz/350g mincemeat

8 floz/240ml milk

3 floz/90ml vegetable oil

3 oz/75g sultanas

icing sugar for dusting

1. Grease muffin tins or insert paper cases.
2. In a large bowl sift together flour, baking powder, bicarbonate of soda, salt and sugar.
3. In a separate bowl beat egg with a fork.
4. Stir in mincemeat, milk and oil.
5. Pour liquid ingredients into dry mixture.
6. Stir until just combined and add sultanas gently. Batter will be lumpy, but no dry flour should be visible. Take care not to over-mix.
7. Fill muffin cups until 3/4 full.
8. Bake until tops are lightly browned and spring back when pressed gently.
9. Allow muffins to cool.
10. Sift icing sugar over tops.

*Margaret Graham, Tarbert, Loch Fyne*

# Coffee Buns

Pre-heat oven to: 180°C/350°F/Gas4 Time in oven: 15-20 minutes Makes: 18

**4 oz/110g margarine**
**6 oz/175g demerara sugar**
**1 egg, beaten**

**2 oz/50g currants**
**8 oz/225g S.R. flour**

1. Melt margarine and add to sugar and egg, leaving enough to paint top of buns.
2. Add currants and flour to make a firm dough.
3. Roll into 18 balls and flatten.
4. Paint top of buns with egg mixture.
5. Bake until golden brown.
6. Enjoy with a mug of coffee!

*Ruth Mackay, St Peter's, Dundee*

# Raspberry Streusel Muffins

Pre-heat oven to: 180°C/350°F/Gas4 Time in oven: 30-35 minutes Makes: 10

**6 oz/175g S.R. flour**
**1 tsp baking powder**
**4 oz/110g caster sugar**
**1 large egg**
**4 oz/110g unsalted butter, melted**
**7 floz/200ml full cream milk or buttermilk**
**5 oz/150g fresh or frozen raspberries**

***Streusel Topping***
**4 oz/110g icing sugar**
**3 oz/75g S.R. flour**
**3 oz/75g unsalted butter, melted**

1. Line muffin tray with 10 muffin cases.
2. Sift flour and baking powder into a bowl and stir in sugar.
3. Add egg, melted butter and milk and stir until combined. The mixture should be lumpy.
4. Fold in raspberries with a large spoon.
5. For the topping, sift icing sugar into a large bowl and stir in flour. Rub in butter until large crumbs form.
6. Spoon muffin batter into each case and drop streusel topping on top of each muffin.
7. Bake until muffins are well risen and golden brown.
8. Serve warm or cold.

*Emma Lipp, Bon Accord, Aberdeen*

# Summer Fruit Muffins

Pre-heat oven to: 190°C/375°F/Gas5     Time in oven: 20-25 mins     Makes: 10-12

| | |
|---|---|
| 10 oz/275g S.R. flour | 1 egg, at room temperature |
| 1 tsp baking powder | 8 floz/250ml milk |
| ½ tsp salt | 3 floz/90ml corn oil |
| 4 oz/110g granulated sugar | 5 oz/150g summer fruit |

Note: Use any berries, either alone or in combination: blueberries, raspberries, blackberries, strawberries, redcurrants, blackcurrants, cherries, fresh or frozen. Do not thaw frozen berries. Larger sized berries should be coarsely chopped.

1. Grease muffin tray or insert paper cases.
2. In large bowl sift together flour, baking powder and salt.
3. Stir in sugar and set aside.
4. In another bowl beat egg with a fork, then stir in milk and oil.
5. Pour all wet ingredients into dry. Stir gently until just combined. There should be no visible flour. The less stirring the better. Mixture will be lumpy.
6. Gently fold in berries at the end, using only 2-3 strokes to avoid crushing fruit.
7. Spoon into cases and place in oven. Frozen fruit will require an extra 4-5 minutes.
8. Muffins are ready when tops are lightly browned and spring back when pressed gently.
9. Try using a mini muffin pan and cases for children, but reduce baking time.

*A Moir, Kirkcaldy*

# Chocolate Fridge Chunks

Makes: 16 squares

10 oz/275g chocolate digestive biscuits or choc chip cookies

3 ½ oz/100g bar good quality white chocolate, roughly chopped

3 ½ oz/100g dried cherries or mix of cherries and raisins

3 ½ oz/100g butter

3 ½ oz/100g plain or milk chocolate, broken into chunks

1. Put biscuits in a strong polythene bag and use end of a rolling pin to crush them roughly into coarse crumbs.
2. Tip into a large bowl and add chopped white chocolate and dried fruit.
3. Slowly heat butter with plain or milk chocolate until just melted.
4. Pour over biscuit mixture and mix well together.
5. Spoon into a greased 8"/20cm square shallow tin.
6. Leave to cool for at least 1 hour in fridge, until firm. Cut into squares.

*Joan M Macleod, Back, Lewis*

# Coconut Delights

Makes: 48 squares

*Base*
1 small can condensed milk
9 oz/250g desiccated coconut
2 tbs icing sugar

*Middle*
1 small can condensed milk
4 oz/110g margarine
4 oz/110g caster sugar
1 tbs syrup

*Topping*
11 oz/300g white chocolate
3/4 small packet Rice Krispies

1. Mix base ingredients together and spread on a greased 9"x13"/23cmx32.5cm baking tray.
2. Boil middle ingredients in pan slowly for 3-4 minutes and beat and pour over base.
3. Melt chocolate, add Rice Krispies and spread on top.
4. Allow to cool and cut into squares.

*Margaret MacIsaac, Smithton-Culloden*

# Date Crispies

Makes: 30 squares

6 oz/175g dates
1 oz/25g glace cherries
1 oz/25g preserved ginger, optional

4 oz/110g margarine or butter
2 oz/50g sugar
2 oz/50g Rice Krispies
6 oz/175g cooking chocolate

1. Chop dates, cherries and ginger.
2. Put chopped fruit, margarine and sugar in a pan.
3. Cook over slow heat until dates are soft. Remove from heat.
4. Add Rice Krispies and mix well. Press into a 11" x 7"/28cm x 18cm baking tray.
5. Cover with melted chocolate. Cut into slices when set.

*Helen Mackay, St Vincent Street/Milton*

# Malteser Crunch

Makes: 32 pieces

4 oz/110g butter
8 oz/225g Cadbury's milk chocolate
3 tbs syrup

8 oz/225g digestive biscuits, crushed
8 oz/225g Maltesers, remove 10 and crush
8 oz/225g Milky Bar white chocolate, melted

1. Melt butter, chocolate and syrup over low heat.
2. Add crushed digestive biscuits and whole Maltesers.
3. Press into a greased 11" x 8"/28cm x 20cm baking tray. Allow to harden.
4. Cover with white chocolate and sprinkle crushed Maltesers on top. Cut when set.

*Mary B Macleod, Knock, Lewis*

# Mallow Fudge Squares

Makes: 24 squares

4 oz/110g butter
11 oz/300g Galaxy chocolate
4 tbs syrup
14 oz/400g digestive biscuits
2 oz/50g raisins
2 oz/50g chopped cherries

11 oz/300g white Scotblock
7 oz/200g mini marshmallows
icing sugar

1. Melt butter and chocolate slowly over low heat.
2. Stir in syrup, biscuits, raisins and cherries.
3. Press firmly into a greased 7"x11"/18cmx28cm baking tray.
4. Melt chocolate and mix in marshmallows. Pour over base and leave in fridge to set.
5. Dust with icing sugar and cut into squares.

*Margaret MacLeod, Lochs, Lewis*

# Marzipan Roll

Makes: 10-12 slices

2 oz/50g margarine
small can condensed milk

14 digestive biscuits, crushed
2 tbs drinking chocolate
8 oz/225g marzipan
2 tbs coconut, optional

1. Melt margarine and condensed milk.
2. Add dry ingredients. Allow to cool slightly.
3. Roll out marzipan and spread mixture over it. Roll up like a swiss roll.
4. Place in fridge until firm. Cut into slices.
5. Store in fridge.

*Catherine Matheson, Kyle*

# No Cook Crunch

Makes: 24 squares

*Base*
4 oz/110g margarine
2 tbs syrup
4 oz/110g cooking chocolate
8 oz/225g digestive biscuits, crushed
2 oz/50g cherries, chopped
2 oz/50g raisins

*Topping*
2 oz/50g butter
4 oz/110g cooking chocolate
6 oz/175g icing sugar

*Base*
1. Melt margarine, syrup and chocolate in pan over gentle heat.
2. Remove from heat and stir in biscuits, cherries and raisins.
3. Press mixture into a greased 7" x 11"/18cm x 28cm baking tray.

*Topping*
1. Melt butter and chocolate and add icing sugar.
2. Spread on to biscuit mixture and leave to cool.
3. Place in fridge and cut into squares when cold.

*Catherine Fraser, Kyle*

# Barley Meal Scones

Makes: 4 bannocks

8 oz/225g barley meal
¹/₂ tsp bicarbonate of soda
I tsp cream of tartar

¹/₂ tsp salt
2 oz/50g sugar
2 oz/50g melted margarine
hot water to make stiff consistency

1. Heat griddle.
2. Mix all ingredients until stiff.
3. Divide into 4 pieces and roll out thin circles on some barley meal.
4. Cook on hot griddle, turning once, until ready.

*Nan Macdonald, Dowanvale, Glasgow*

119

# Buttermilk Scones with Raspberry and White Chocolate

Pre-heat oven to: 220°C/425°F/Gas7     Time in oven: 10-12 minutes     Makes: 16

1 lb/450g S.R. soda bread flour
3 oz/75g margarine
3 oz/75g caster sugar

3 oz/75g white chocolate buttons
1 large egg, beaten
1/2 pt/300ml buttermilk
16 raspberries, fresh or frozen

1. Sift flour into bowl and rub in margarine until mixture resembles breadcrumbs. Add sugar.
2. Break white chocolate into smaller pieces and add to mixture.
3. Add beaten egg and enough buttermilk to bring mixture together. It should be soft but not sticky.
4. Form dough into a ball and place on a lightly floured surface. Roll into a circle at least 1" /2.5cm thick.
5. Using a 2 1/2"/6cm cutter, cut out scones and place on a lightly floured baking tray.
6. Make a small hollow in centre of each scone and push a raspberry into dough.
7. Brush top lightly with milk or dust with some caster sugar.
8. Bake until golden brown. Remove to wire rack to cool.
9. Serve warm with butter.

*Note: If unable to purchase soda bread flour, S.R. flour can be used. These scones freeze well and should be frozen if not used within 1-2 days.*

*Ruth Beattie, Groomsport, E.PC., N.Ireland*

# Cressington Soda Bread

Pre-heat oven to: 190°C/375°F/Gas5     Time in oven: 1 hour in total     Serves: 12

8 oz/225g plain flour
8 oz/225g wholemeal plain flour
1 tsp bicarbonate of soda
2 tsp cream of tartar
1 tbs caster sugar
1/2 tsp salt

1 tbs olive oil
8 oz/225g natural yoghurt
1/4 pt/150ml milk

1. In a large bowl sift together the flours, bicarbonate of soda, cream of tartar, sugar and salt.
2. Mix together olive oil and yoghurt and stir into dry ingredients with a wooden spoon, adding enough milk to make a soft dough.
3. Place dough in a greased and lined 2 lb/900g loaf tin, bake for 45 minutes then turn oven down to 180°C/350°F/Gas4 for another 15 minutes.
4. Leave to cool for 2 minutes then turn out on to cooling tray.

*Sheena Berry, Dowanvale, Glasgow*

# Wholemeal Bonnach

Pre-heat oven to: 180°C/305°F/Gas4     Time in oven: 25-30 mins     Serves: 10-12

**8 oz/225g plain wholemeal flour**     **1 oz/25g butter**
**8 oz/225g plain flour**     **8 floz/250ml milk**
**1 tbs bicarbonate of soda**
**1 tsp cream of tartar**
**pinch of salt**

1. Sieve all dry ingredients into bowl. Rub in butter with finger tips until mixture looks like breadcrumbs.
2. Add milk and mix to form a soft dough. Knead on floured surface for 2 minutes.
3. Form into a circle about 1"/2.5cm thick.
4. Place on floured baking tray and place in oven.
5. Bake until risen and well browned. Cool on a wire rack.

*Note: Excellent with home-made soup.*

*Fiona MacLean, Leverburgh*

# Savoury Herb Scones

Pre-heat oven to: 200°C/400°F/Gas 6     Time in oven: 15 minutes     Makes: 8

**4 oz/110g potatoes, cooked and sieved**     **1 tbs parsley, chopped**
**4 oz/110g S.R. flour**     **1 tbs chives, chopped**
**3 oz/75g lard, or any fat**     **1 medium egg**
**good pinch of salt**     **milk**
**good pinch of cayenne pepper**     **2 oz/50g corn flakes, crushed**

1. Mix together cooled potatoes and flour.
2. Rub in fat until mixture resembles fine breadcrumbs.
3. Add salt, cayenne pepper, parsley and chives.
4. Beat egg and milk, reserving a little for brushing on scones at end.
5. Add egg and enough milk to make a soft dough.
6. Roll out dough to a 1/2"/1cm thick oblong shape.
7. Sprinkle crushed corn flakes over top.
8. Roll dough up like a large sausage, cut into even slices and flatten slightly with your hand.
9. Brush over with a little of beaten egg and milk.
10. Bake in oven until nicely risen and golden in colour.

*Note: Best with floury potatoes.*

*Mary Noble, Tarbert*

# Quick Wholemeal Scones

Pre-heat oven to: 200°C/400°F/Gas6     Time in oven: 10 minutes     Makes: 10-12

1 lb/450g S.R. wholemeal flour

2 tsp baking powder

2 tbs granulated sugar

2 tbs oil, or melted butter

milk to mix

1. Mix together flour, baking powder, sugar and oil with enough milk to form a soft dough.
2. Turn dough on to floured surface and flatten by hand until 1"/2.5cm thick.
3. Use pastry cutter or small cup to press out circles of dough.
4. Place on floured baking tray and bake until well risen and brown. Cool on wire rack.

*Rosina Murray, Dornoch*

# Oatcakes

Pre-heat oven to: 180°C/350°F/Gas4     Time in oven: 15-20 minutes     Makes: 36

8 oz/225g S.R. flour

1 level tsp bicarbonate of soda

1 lb/450g pinhead oatmeal, medium

1 tsp salt

5 oz/150g margarine or butter

3 floz/90ml water

2 tbs milk

1. Mix together dry ingredients in bowl and rub in margarine until mixture resembles fine breadcrumbs.
2. Stir in water and milk combination.
3. Sift some flour on work surface and roll out dough thinly. Cut into circles of 2"/5cm diameter and lift on to baking tray.
4. Bake until golden brown.
5. Cool on wire tray until cold. Store in air tight container.

*Note: To freshen 4-day-old cakes, heat in moderate oven for 3-5 minutes.*

*Mina Patterson, Greenock*

# Sweet Oatcakes

Pre-heat oven to: 180°C/350°F/Gas4     Time in oven: 15-20 minutes     Makes: 12

4 oz/110g S.R. flour

4 oz/110g medium oatmeal

2 oz/50g caster sugar

4 oz/110g margarine

1. Mix all dry ingredients together and rub in margarine.
2. Knead together and roll out. Cut into rounds and place on a greased tray.
3. Bake in oven.

*Janet Macleod, Helmsdale*

# Oil Pancakes

Makes: 12-16

| | |
|---|---|
| 6 heaped tbs S.R. flour | 2 eggs |
| 2 tsp baking powder | 2 tbs oil |
| pinch of salt | 2 tsp syrup |
| 4 heaped tbs caster sugar | 8 floz/250ml milk |

1. Sieve flour, baking powder and salt into a mixing bowl and add sugar
2. Mix eggs and oil together and stir in syrup and milk.
3. Make a well in centre, stir in half milk mixture, add remainder and stir well, aiming for dropping consistency.
4. Drop mixture in spoonfuls on a greased pre-heated griddle over low heat.
5. When ready, turn over and brown second side.
6. Cool in a tea towel on cooling tray.

*Jessie Mackenzie, Rosskeen*

# Apricot Loaf

Pre-heat oven to: 170°C/325°F/Gas3       Time in oven: 1 hr 10 mins       Serves: 12-20

| | |
|---|---|
| 3 oz/75g glacé cherries | 4 oz/110g sultanas |
| 2 oz/50g blanched almonds | grated rind of 1 orange |
| 4 oz/110g dried apricots | 4 oz/110g Muscovado sugar |
| | 6 oz/175g S.R. flour |
| | pinch of salt |
| | 4 oz/110g margarine, melted |
| | 2 eggs, beaten |

1. Place cherries in colander and pour boiling water over to get rid of their sugary coating. Dry with kitchen paper and chop. Reserve 1 tbs chopped cherries for decoration.
2. Roughly chop apricots and almonds. Reserve 1-2 apricots for decoration.
3. Combine all dry ingredients in large mixing bowl.
4. Add margarine and eggs. When thoroughly combined, spoon into a greased and lined 2 lb/900g loaf tin. Bake in centre of oven.
5. When cool, loaf can be iced if desired.
6. Cover top of cake with a thin coating of apricot jam and fondant or glacé icing. (See Apple and Walnut Cake on page no 105)
7. Decorate with chopped apricots and cherries.
8. May be eaten as a cake or sliced and buttered.

*Nina MacLeod, Portmahomack, Inverness*

# All Bran Loaf
Pre-heat oven to: 180°C/350°F/Gas4      Time in oven: 1 hour      Makes: 10 slices

1 cup All Bran

1 cup dried fruit

1 cup brown sugar

1 cup milk

1 tbs sherry, optional

1 cup S.R. flour

1 egg, beaten

1. Combine All Bran, dried fruit, brown sugar, milk and sherry. Soak in bowl for 1 hour.
2. Beat in egg and flour.
3. Spoon mixture into a greased and lined 1 lb/450g loaf tin and bake in oven.
4. Remove from tin and cool on wire rack.

*Mary Sutherland, Urray & Strathconon*

# Fruit Loaf
Pre-heat oven to: 180°C/350°F/Gas4      Time in oven: 45 mins    Makes: 12-20 slices

4 oz/110g butter

1/4 pt/150ml water

4 oz/110g raisins

4 oz/110g sultanas

4 oz/110g caster sugar

8 oz/225g S.R. flour

2 eggs, well beaten

2 level tsp bicarbonate of soda

1. Melt butter in medium sized pan then add water, raisins and sultanas.
2. Boil for 2 minutes, add all other ingredients and mix well.
3. Place in a greased and lined 2 lb/900g loaf tin.
4. Bake in oven until well risen and top of loaf springs back when pressed gently in the middle.
5. Cool and serve, spread with butter.

*M. MacKinnon, Waternish, Skye*

# Julie's Banana Loaf
Pre-heat oven to: 350°F/180°C/Gas4      Time in oven: 30 minutes    Makes: 20 slices

6 oz/175g caster sugar

4 oz/110g margarine

2 eggs, beaten

2 bananas, mashed

1 tsp bicarbonate of soda

2 tsp boiling milk

8 oz/225g S.R. flour

1 tsp baking powder

1. Cream sugar and margarine and stir in eggs and bananas.
2. Combine bicarbonate of soda and boiling milk and add to banana mix.
3. Sift flour and baking powder and fold into mixture until smooth.
4. Pour into two greased 1 lb/450g loaf tins and bake in oven until golden brown.

*Note: Do not throw out over-ripe bananas - freeze, defrost and use in baking recipes.*

*Chris Nicolson, Castletown*

# American Nut Chocolate Brownies

Pre-heat oven to: 180°C/350°F/Gas4     Time in oven: 30 minutes     Makes: 12-18

4 oz/110g nuts mixed e.g. pecan,       2 oz/50g plain flour
brazil, walnut, macadamia, not peanut    1 tsp baking powder
2 oz/50g dark chocolate          ¹/₄ tsp salt
4 oz/110g butter            6 oz/175g granulated sugar
                       2 large eggs

1. Toast nuts slightly on tray in oven for 15 minutes and chop into chunks.
2. Melt chocolate and butter over hot water and beat.
3. Add all other ingredients and mix well.
4. Line an oblong 7" x 11"/18cm x 28cm tin with baking parchment and spread mixture over evenly.
5. Place in oven and bake. Brownies should be springy on top when ready.
6. Leave to cool for 10 minutes, then cut up still in the tin into large squares and lift each out on to a cooling tray.

*Note: This is not a cake. The inside will be, and should be, soft - even damp, and crisp on the outside. It will shrink a little as it cools.*

*Catriona Neilson, Sleat and Strath, Skye*

# Gairloch Shortbread

Pre-heat oven to: 180C°/350°F/Gas4     Time in oven: 40 mins     Makes: 21 fingers

4 oz/110g margarine          *Icing*
2 oz/50g caster sugar        2 oz/50g margarine
5 oz/125g plain flour        4 level tbs icing sugar
1 oz/25g cornflour          3 level tbs syrup
                       1 level tsp cinnamon or ginger

*Shortbread*
1. Beat margarine and sugar to a soft cream.
2. Add sifted flour and cornflour and mix well.
3. Press mixture into a greased 7"/18cm square sandwich tin.
4. Bake until golden brown.

*Icing*
1. Gently mix all ingredients together over low heat, until thoroughly blended.
2. Pour over shortbread while still warm.
3. Cut into fingers when cold.

*Sena Leitch, Thurso*

# Flapjacks

Pre-heat oven to: 170°C/325°F/Gas3 Time in oven: 15-20 mins Makes: 24 squares

5 oz/150g margarine
5 oz/150g Muscovado sugar
½ tsp vanilla essence

6 oz/175g porridge oats
2 oz/50g oatmeal
2 oz/50g dates, optional
2 oz/50g wholemeal flour

1. Beat margarine, sugar and vanilla essence together.
2. Mix in oats, oatmeal, dates and brown flour.
3. Press into a greased 7" x 11"/18cm x 28cm baking tray and bake.
4. Take out of oven and cut into squares. Leave to cool in tin.

*Jean Allan, Arran*

# Florentine Slices

Pre-heat oven to: 170°C/325°F/Gas3 Time in oven: 45 minutes Makes: 12

8 oz/225g block chocolate broken into pieces
2 oz/50g butter
4 oz/110g brown sugar
1 egg, beaten

2 oz/50g sultanas or raisins
4 oz/110g coconut
2 oz/50g cherries, quartered

1. Melt chocolate over hot water until melted, stirring occasionally.
2. Spoon chocolate into a 7"/18cm square sponge tin, spread evenly and leave to harden.
3. Cream butter and sugar until fluffy then beat in egg thoroughly.
4. Mix together remaining ingredients and add to creamed mixture.
5. Spoon into tin and spread over chocolate.
6. Bake in centre of oven until golden brown. Leave for 5 minutes and mark with knife.
7. When cold, remove from tin.

*Katie MacKenzie, Bracadale, Skye*

# Fruity Chocolate Chip Squares

Pre-heat oven to: 180°C/350°F/Gas4     Time in oven: 25-30 minutes     Makes: 16

5 oz/150g butter or margarine

5 oz/150g golden caster sugar

3 eggs

7 oz/200g S.R. flour

3 tbs milk

3 ¹/₂ oz/100g glacé cherries, chopped

2 oz/50g dried apricots, chopped

2 oz/50g dates or sultanas, chopped

3 ¹/₂ oz/100g packet chocolate chips

golden caster sugar, for sprinkling

1. Cream butter and sugar until light and fluffy.
2. Beat in eggs one at a time with 1 tbs flour. Fold in remainder of flour.
3. Add milk, fruit and chocolate chips and mix well. Bake in oven.
4. Leave to cool for 5 minutes before removing from tin.
5. When cold, cut into squares and sprinkle with a little golden caster sugar.

*Catherine MacDonald, Carloway*

# French Country Bars

Pre-heat oven to: 180°C/350°F/Gas 4     Time in oven: 45 minutes     Makes: 24

6 oz/175g block margarine

6 oz/175g wholemeal plain flour

2 tsp baking powder

6 oz/175g mixed dried fruit

8 oz/225g soft brown sugar

2 oz/50g chopped mixed nuts, optional

2 ¹/₂ oz/60g porridge oats

1 egg, beaten

1. Grease and line a 7" x 11"/18cm x 28cm baking tray with a little of the margarine.
2. Melt remainder of margarine slowly.
3. Place remaining dry ingredients in bowl and mix.
4. Stir in melted margarine and egg.
5. Spoon mixture on to prepared tin and press down evenly using the back of a spoon.
6. Bake in oven.
7. Cool in tin and cut into squares.

*Sheena Berry, Dowanvale*

# Helen's Squares

Pre-heat oven to: 190°C/375°F/Gas5     Time in oven: 30 mins     Makes: 36 squares

| | |
|---|---|
| **4 oz/110g butter or margarine** | **Icing** |
| **2 oz/50g sugar** | **3 level tbs sugar** |
| **I egg** | **3 tbs butter** |
| **I dsp syrup** | **2 tbs milk** |
| **3 oz/75g coconut** | **I tsp vanilla essence** |
| **5 oz/150g sultanas** | **3-4 tbs icing sugar** |
| **4 ¹/₂ oz/125g plain flour** | |
| **I tsp baking powder** | |

*Base*
1. Cream butter and sugar together then add egg, syrup, coconut and sultanas.
2. Add dry ingredients and mix together well.
3. Press into a 12" x 10"/30cm x 25.5cm greased tin.
4. Bake in oven and ice when cold.

*Icing*
1. Boil sugar, butter and milk together for 3 minutes. Remove from heat and beat.
2. Add vanilla essence and icing sugar.
3. Pour over base and cut into squares when cold.

*Elsie MacKenzie, Keiss*

---

# Peppermint Slice

Pre-heat oven to: 180°C/350°F/Gas4     Time in oven: 20-25 mins     Makes: 48 squares

| | |
|---|---|
| **Base** | **Topping** |
| **8 oz/225g margarine** | **8 oz/225g icing sugar** |
| **6 oz/175g plain flour** | **2-3 dsp milk** |
| **4 oz/110g caster sugar** | **2 tsp peppermint essence** |
| **6 oz/175g coconut** | **I tsp green colouring** |
| **5 tsp cocoa** | **8 oz/225g chocolate** |
| **I tsp baking powder** | |

1. Rub margarine into flour until mixture resembles fine breadcrumbs.
2. Add sugar, coconut, cocoa and baking powder.
3. Press into a greased 13" x 9"/32.5cm x 23cms baking tray and bake. Allow to cool.
4. Mix together sugar, milk, essence and colouring and spread over base.
5. Melt chocolate and pour over green icing.
6. When chocolate hardens cut into squares.

*Connie Thomson, East Kilbride*

# Lemon Squares
Pre-heat oven to: 180°C/350°F/Gas4 Time in oven: 40-45 mins in total Makes: 24

8 oz/225g plain flour
2 oz/50g icing sugar
¼ tsp salt
6 oz/175g cold butter or margarine
1 tsp cold water

*Lemon Layer*
4 eggs
1 lb/450g caster sugar
1 oz/25g plain flour
½ tsp baking powder
1 tsp grated lemon rind
2 floz/50ml fresh lemon juice
icing sugar for sprinkling

1. Sift flour, icing sugar and salt into a bowl.
2. Using finger tips, rub in butter until mix is like coarse breadcrumbs.
3. Add water and stir lightly with fork until mix forms a ball.
4. Press into an ungreased 13" x 9"/32cm x 23cm baking dish. Bake for 15-20 minutes, until brown. Leave to cool.
5. Beat together eggs, caster sugar, flour, baking powder, lemon juice and rind.
6. Pour lemon mixture over baked base, return to oven and bake for 25 minutes.
7. Leave to cool in dish, sprinkle top with icing sugar and cut into squares.

*Caroline Campbell, Lonemore, Skye*

# Magic Bars
Pre-heat oven to: 180°C/350°F/Gas4 Time in oven: 25 to 30 mins Makes: 36 bars

4 oz/110g butter or hard margarine
6 oz/175g digestive biscuit crumbs

10 floz/300ml condensed milk
6 oz/175g chocolate chips
4 oz/110g desiccated coconut
1 teacup chopped walnuts

1. Melt butter or margarine in a 9" x 13"/23cm x 32cm baking tin.
2. Sprinkle digestive biscuit crumbs over butter in pan.
3. Carefully spread condensed milk over top, trying to get it as even as possible.
4. Sprinkle chocolate chips over top, followed by coconut and walnuts.
5. With your hand, press down lightly all over. Bake until light brown.
6. Cut when cool.

*Margaret MacAulay, Cross, Lewis*

# New Zealand Louise Cake

Pre-heat oven to: 180°C/350°F/Gas4     Time in oven: 30 mins     Makes: 20-24 slices

2 ½ oz/60g butter
5 oz/150g caster sugar
2 eggs

5 oz/150g plain flour
½ tsp baking powder
raspberry jam
2 oz/50g desiccated coconut

1. Cream butter and 1 oz/25g sugar.
2. Separate eggs and add yolks to creamed mixture.
3. Stir in flour and baking powder.
4. Spread mixture on a greased 8" x 11"/20cm x 28cm baking tray and cover with thin layer of raspberry jam.
5. Beat egg whites until stiff and fold in remainder of sugar and coconut.
6. Cover raspberry jam with meringue and bake in oven.
7. Cut into slices when cool.

*Ann Johnson, Dumbarton*

# Sultana Slice

Pre-heat oven to: 170°C/325°F/Gas3     Time in oven: 1 hour     Makes: 24

1 lb/450g sultanas
8 oz/225g margarine

3 eggs
12 oz/350g caster sugar
2 tsp almond essence
12 oz/350g plain flour
2 tsp baking powder

1. Place sultanas in pan, cover with water, bring to the boil and simmer for 10 minutes.
2. Drain sultanas, stir in margarine and allow to melt.
3. Whisk together eggs, sugar and essence. Add sultanas and margarine and mix.
4. Fold in sifted flour and baking powder.
5. Pour into a greased and base-lined 9" x 11"/23cm x 28cm deep baking tray, smooth surface with a palette knife and bake in oven.
6. Turn on to a cooling tray. When cold, cover with sifted icing sugar and cut into squares or rectangles.

*Ann Smith, Bon Accord, Aberdeen*

 **preserves**

## Blackcurrant Jam

4 lbs/1.8 kg blackcurrants       5 ½ lbs/2.5 kg sugar

2 ½ pts/1.5 litre water

1. Wash and stalk fruit and simmer very slowly in water until skins are tender, about 45 minutes.
2. Add sugar, stir until boiling and boil rapidly.
3. Test after 10 minutes. Jam should be set within 15 minutes of boiling.
4. Put into warm sterilized jars.

*Joan Matheson, Lochbroom*

## Rhubarb & Orange Jam

4 lbs/1.8 kg rhubarb       1 orange

1 dsp ground ginger       4 lbs/1.8 kg granulated sugar

1. Cut up rhubarb, place in bowl and add ginger.
2. Remove orange peel, slice flesh and add to bowl.
3. Pour sugar over and leave to soak overnight.
4. Transfer to jam pan and bring to the boil, stirring from time to time.
5. Test for setting after about 40 minutes.
6. Cool, put into jars and cover.

*Irene Chisholm, Inverasdale*

## Sweet Chutney

2 lb/900g cooking apples, peeled and cored       8 oz/225g brown sugar

8 oz/225g sultanas       1 tsp salt

8 oz/225g cooking dates, chopped       1 tsp cayenne pepper

8 oz/225g onions       1 tsp ground pepper

½ pt/300ml vinegar       1 tsp ground nutmeg

1. Boil apples, sultanas, dates and onion in vinegar to a pulp.
2. Add sugar, salt and spices and simmer for further 15 minutes.
3. Pot and seal when cold.

*Jane de la Haye, Wick*

# Tomato Relish

| | |
|---|---|
| 5 large onions, peeled and chopped | 2 tbs pickling spices, in cloth or muslin bag |
| 18 floz/500ml white vinegar | 1 lb/450g sugar |
| 12 large ripe tomatoes, peeled and chopped | 1 tbs salt |
| | 2 green peppers, peeled and chopped |

1. Cook onions in vinegar until soft.
2. Add tomatoes, spices in bag, sugar, salt and green pepper.
3. Boil until thick, for approximately 2-2 1/2 hrs, stirring often.
4. Bottle when cold.

*Margaret Shaw, Desable, Prince Edward Island*

# Apricot Chutney

Makes: 8-9 lbs/4kg

| | |
|---|---|
| 1 lb 2 oz/500g dried apricots | 1 lb 2 oz/500g sultanas |
| 1 lb 12 oz/800g onions | 2 lb 4 oz/1 kg sugar |
| | 28 floz/800ml vinegar |
| | 4 level tsp salt |
| | 1 tsp crushed black peppercorns |
| | 1 tsp nutmeg |

1. Chop apricots and onions finely and put in large bowl.
2. Add remaining ingredients.
3. Stir well, cover and leave for 24 hours, stirring occasionally.
4. Pot.

*Note: Best left for a day or two before using.*

*I.M. Little, Dunblane*

# Carrot Jam

| | |
|---|---|
| 1 lb/450g sugar to each 1 lb/450g of carrots | 2 tbs brandy to each 1 lb/450g pulp |
| juice of 2 lemons to each 1 lb/450g pulp | |

1. Wash and skin carrots and cut in to small pieces.
2. Place in thick-based pan with barely sufficient water to cover and simmer gently until tender.
3. Drain well and liquidize or press through fine sieve.
4. Weigh pulp and return to pan. Add equal amounts of sugar and lemon juice.
5. Bring slowly to the boil. Boil for 15 minutes, remove from heat and add brandy.
6. Pour into small jars, cover and store in dry cool place.

*Note: Unless brandy is added jam will not keep.*

*Joan Mackenzie, Park, Lewis*

 # microwave

## After Eight Cake

Serves: 8

8 oz/225g chocolate digestives
3 oz/75g butter or margarine

1 box After Eights
10 floz/300ml extra thick double cream

1. Melt margarine, crush digestives and mix together.
2. Press into a greased 8½"/20cm flan or quiche dish.
3. Melt After Eights in microwave at 600W for short bursts of 20 seconds, stirring in between so they do not burn.
4. Allow to cool before whisking in cream.
5. Pour over biscuit base and chill in fridge before serving.

*Aileen Macleod, Urray & Strathconnon*

## Chocolate Sponge

Serves: 8-10

*Sponge*
3 oz/75g soft tub margarine
5 oz/150g soft light brown sugar
2 eggs
4 oz/110g sifted S.R. flour
1 oz/25g sifted cocoa powder
½ level tsp baking powder
3 tbs milk

*Butter-cream Filling*
3 oz/75g butter
6 oz/175g icing sugar
½ oz/10g cocoa powder
1 tbs milk

1. Place all sponge ingredients in mixing bowl and beat for 2-3 minutes until light and fluffy.
2. Place in a greased and lined 8"/20cm microwave dish and level with palette knife.
3. Microwave on high for 5-6 minutes. Leave to cool.
4. Beat butter until soft and sift in icing sugar, cocoa powder, and milk.
5. Beat until fluffy.
6. Split sponge, use half mixture for filling and half to decorate top.

*C. Jessie Sinclair, Dingwall.*

# Date and Apple Chutney

| | |
|---|---|
| 1 1/2 lb/700g cooking apples | 4 oz/110g sultanas |
| 1 lb/450g stoned dates, chopped | 1 tsp salt |
| 8 oz/225g onions, finely chopped | 1 tsp ground ginger |
| 8 oz/225g soft dark brown sugar | 1/2 tsp cayenne pepper |
| | 1 pt/600ml malt vinegar |

1. Peel, core and chop apples. Place in large microwaveable bowl.
2. Cover and microwave at 650W for 5 minutes or until apples reduce in volume.
3. Add remaining ingredients to apples in bowl.
4. Cover and microwave at 650W for 30 to 40 minutes, or until thickened, stirring every 10 minutes.
5. Leave to cool slightly and ladle into sterilized, warmed jars.
6. Cover, seal and label.

*Note: Makes about 4 1/2 lb/2kg*

*Anonymous, Brora*

# Lemon Curd

| | |
|---|---|
| 3 oz/75g butter | 4 good sized lemons |
| 14 oz/400g granulated sugar | 4 medium eggs, well beaten |

1. Grate lemon rind and squeeze out juice.
2. Melt butter in glass or plastic bowl in microwave at 800W for 1 minute.
3. Add sugar and reheat at 600W for 3 minutes, stirring once or twice.
4. Add lemon rind and juice to butter and sugar mixture.
5. Return to microwave and bring to near boiling at 600W for about 3 minutes, stirring every half minute.
6. Add beaten eggs to mixture and stir thoroughly.
7. Reheat at 600W, stirring every half minute until appropriate thickness is reached.
8. Put into jars and keep in fridge.

*Donald Mackay, Golspie*

# Clootie Dumpling

Serves: 8

5 floz/150ml water
4 oz/110g brown sugar
4 oz/110g margarine
8 oz/225g sultanas
1/2 tsp bicarbonate soda
1 dsp treacle

4 oz/110g S.R. flour
2 tsp cinnamon
1 egg, beaten

1. Gently melt first 6 ingredients together in microwave at 600W for 2 minutes. Do not allow to become hot.
2. Add flour, cinnamon and egg and mix well.
3. Put in 2 pt/1.2 litre pyrex bowl lined with clingfilm and cover with plate.
4. Cook in microwave at 800W for 6 minutes.
5. Remove from microwave and allow to cool for 5 minutes. Turn on to serving plate.

*Effie Lamont, Glenelg*

# Raspberry Jam

1 lb/450g raspberries, frozen          1 lb/450g granulated sugar

1. Microwave raspberries at high in large bowl for 5 minutes.
2. Add sugar and stir.
3. Return to microwave and cook at high for further 10 minutes.
4. Stir, put into sterilized jars and cover.

*Connie Beaton, Tain*

# Tablet

1 lb/450g caster sugar          1 small can evaporated milk
2 oz/50g butter

1. Place ingredients in large bowl and microwave at 800W for 2-3 minutes.
2. Remove from microwave and stir well.
3. Return to microwave and cook for further 5 minutes at 800W.
4. Remove from microwave and stir for about 1 minute until mixture thickens.
5. Place in buttered tray and mark when cold.

*Cena Gray, Dowanvale, Glasgow*

# Poacher's Pouch

Serves: 1

1 salmon steak
1/2 red pepper, cut into strips
1/2 green pepper, cut into strips
1/2 carrot, cut into strips
3 spring onions, finely sliced

juice of 1/2 orange
2 tbs soya sauce
salt and pepper

1. Place salmon steak on greaseproof paper on microwaveable plate.
2. Place peppers, carrot and spring onions on top of salmon.
3. Mix together orange juice and soya sauce and pour over. Season.
4. Gather edges of greaseproof paper together to form parcel shape.
5. Place in microwave on high for 5-6 minutes.
6. Allow to stand for 30 seconds.
7. Serve with mashed potatoes and hollandaise sauce.

*M. Macleay, Barvas, Lewis*

# Quickest Ever Fish Pie

Serves: 4

14 oz/400g smoked haddock
1 leek, trimmed and thinly sliced
chopped parsley

5 floz/150ml double cream
2 medium baking potatoes

1. Skin haddock and cut into chunks.
2. Scatter haddock, leek and parsley on base of shallow dish suitable for grill and microwave and mix together.
3. Drizzle over half the cream and 4 tbs water.
4. Wash potatoes, leave skin on and slice thinly. Lay potato slices over fish and leeks and drizzle over remaining cream.
5. Season potato slices with salt and plenty of black pepper.
6. Put grill on high.
7. Cover dish with clingfilm and pierce a few times.
8. Microwave pie on highest setting for 8-10 minutes, until everything is bubbling and potatoes are tender.
9. Remove clingfilm and put dish under grill, until potatoes are golden.
10. Leave to rest for 1 minute and serve straight from dish.

*Note: If desired, grated cheese, breadcrumbs or tomatoes can be added as a topping prior to grilling.*

*Donna Macleod, Knock, Lewis*

# miscellaneous

## Balsamic Onions

Serves: 4

1 oz/25g butter
3 onions, sliced

2 tbs clear honey
2 tsp mixed herbs
2 floz/55ml balsamic vinegar
$^1/_2$ pt/300 ml vegetable stock

1. Melt butter in pan and fry onions for 10 minutes until soft.
2. Add honey, herbs, vinegar and stock.
3. Simmer for 15 minutes until most of liquid evaporates. Serve hot.

*Catriona MacKay, Cross, Ness, Lewis*

## Shortcrust Pastry

8 oz/225g plain flour
4 oz/110g block margarine

$^1/_4$ tsp salt
cold water

1. Place flour in bowl.
2. Use margarine straight from refrigerator, cut into cubes and rub into flour until mixture resembles breadcrumbs. Add salt.
3. Combine mixture with cold water to make stiff dough. Use as required.

### Baking Blind

Pre-heat oven to: 200°C/400°F/Gas6          Time in oven: 15-16 minutes in total

1. Roll out pastry on floured surface, line suitable tin and prick base with fork. Put in refrigerator for 20 minutes.
2. Cut out piece of greaseproof paper slightly larger than tin. Place over pastry and fill with baking beans/dry pasta.
3. Place tin on baking sheet and bake for 10 minutes. Remove from oven and discard paper and beans.
4. Return to oven until golden for 5-6 minutes. Use as required.

# Parsnip Purée

Serves: 8

3 lb/l.35kg parsnips
salt and pepper

3 oz/75g butter
5 floz/150ml double cream
nutmeg

1. Chop parsnips, boil until soft, and season.
2. When cooked, drain and dry on low heat.
3. Put parsnips in food processor and add butter, cream and nutmeg.
4. Remove from processor and place in pan over low heat until warmed through.
5. Serve with meal.

*Note: Can be made in advance and warmed in oven. Any left over can be used next day mashed into potatoes and fried up. This is a lovely way to eat parsnips.*

*Emia St'Clair Macleod, Kinloch, Lewis*

# Mayonnaise without Eggs

1 level tsp mustard
2 tsp sugar
1/2 tsp salt
pinch of pepper

1 small can evaporated milk
1/2 pt/300ml olive oil
2 tbs wine vinegar

1. Put mustard into bowl with sugar, salt and large pinch of pepper.
2. Add evaporated milk and mix.
3. Beat olive oil in very slowly.
4. Stir in vinegar. The mixture will thicken. Season to taste.

*Kitty MacLeod, Lochs, Lewis*

# White Sauce

**Pouring**
1/2 oz/10g margarine
1/2 oz/10g plain flour
1/2 pt/300ml milk
salt and pepper

**Coating**
1 oz/25g margarine
1 oz/25g plain flour
1/2 pt/300ml milk
salt and pepper

1. Place margarine in pan, melt, stir in flour and cook over gentle heat for 1 minute.
2. Remove from heat, gradually add milk and stir until combined.
3. Replace on heat and bring to boil, stirring constantly. Allow to simmer for 2-3 minutes. Season.

*Note: For cheese sauce, grate 2 oz/50g cheddar cheese and add to sauce once it has simmered.*

# Mayonnaise

| | |
|---|---|
| 2 egg yolks | 1/2 tsp salt |
| 2 tbs white wine vinegar | 1/2 tsp mustard |
| 1 1/2 tsp sugar | 1/2 pint/300ml sunflower oil |

1. Using an electric mixer or blender, whisk together all ingredients except oil.
2. Very slowly and gradually add oil, only a trickle at first, until mixture is blended.

Note: Different wine vinegars can be used, such as garlic, tarragon or raspberry.

*Ishbel Buck, Dowanvale, Glasgow*

# Chocolate Mint Crisps

| | |
|---|---|
| 1 lb/450g plain dark chocolate | 8 ozs/225g demerara sugar |
| | 2 tsp peppermint essence |

1. Chop chocolate in pieces and put in bowl over pan of simmering water until melted.
2. Stir sugar and peppermint essence into chocolate and spread over greaseproof paper.
3. When cool, cut as required.

*Lily M. Campbell, Stornoway, Lewis*

# Fudge

| | |
|---|---|
| 4 oz/110g margarine or unsalted butter | pinch of cream of tartar |
| 1 lb/450g granulated sugar | few drops vanilla essence |
| 5 floz/150ml evaporated milk | |

1. Melt margarine or butter in heavy-based saucepan over gentle heat.
2. Add sugar, evaporated milk, cream of tartar and vanilla essence.
3. Stir gently until sugar has dissolved. Should take about 15 minutes.
4. Bring to the boil slowly and allow to bubble for about 15-20 minutes, stirring gently so it does not stick to bottom of pan.
5. Take pan off heat and beat fudge for 2 minutes.
6. Pour into greased 7"/18cm square tin, allow to cool for 10-15 minutes and mark squares on top.
7. Allow to cool completely before cutting squares.

*Christine Kennedy, Park, Lewis*

# Raspberry Sauce

| | |
|---|---|
| 8 oz/225g raspberries | 4 tbs icing sugar |
| | 1 tbs orange liqueur |

1. Process ingredients in blender and sieve to remove seeds.
2. Chill.

Note: Store in fridge and use within 3 days.

*Marie C. Gillies, Stornoway, Lewis*

**139**

# Roasted Mediterranean Vegetables

Pre-heat oven to: 200°C/400°F/Gas6      Time in oven: 45-60 minutes      Serves: 6

3 tbs olive oil

2 large red onions

4 peppers, red, yellow or orange

2 leeks

$^1/_2$ fennel bulb

2 cloves garlic, chopped

salt and freshly ground black pepper

*Note: Vegetables can be varied, use sweet potatoes and aubergines*

1. Drizzle roasting tin with 1 tbs oil.
2. Chop vegetables into large pieces and spread over tin.
3. Add garlic, salt and pepper.
4. Drizzle over remaining oil and mix thoroughly. Roast in oven.

*Note: Can be cooked at same time as roast beef, lamb, pork etc.*

*Christine Macdonald, Dunblane*

# Yorkshire Puddings

Pre-heat oven to: 220°C/425°F/Gas7.      Time in oven: 15-20 minutes      Makes: 12

2 tbs vegetable oil

4 oz/110g plain flour

2 eggs

$^1/_2$ pt/300ml milk

salt and pepper

1. Place a little oil in each section of muffin tray and place in oven to heat.
2. Sift flour into bowl and whisk in eggs, milk and seasoning to form a smooth batter. Pour into jug.
3. When oil is very hot remove tray carefully from oven and pour batter into 12 sections of tray.
4. Return tray to oven and bake until puddings are well risen and golden brown.

*Dina Macleod, Barvas, Lewis*

# Glazed Carrots

Serves: 4

4 large carrots

2 tbs butter

$^1/_4$ cup brown sugar

3 tbs orange juice

1 tsp grated rind

$^1/_2$ tsp lemon juice

$^1/_4$ tsp ginger

1. Wash, peel and slice carrots.
2. Boil for 2 minutes until just tender, drain and leave to one side.
3. Put remaining ingredients in pan.
4. Stir well and bring to the boil.
5. Add carrots and simmer until cooked and glazed.

*Marjorie Hunter, Brora*

# index

# index

**notes**